TENACITY
of PURPOSE

Coach Preston Goldfarb's Journey through life, loves and soccer

D1517809

PRESTON GOLDFARB
With Scott Adamson

Charleston, SC

www.PalmettoPublishing.com

First Edition

ISBN: 978-1-63837-949-2

Front cover image courtesy of RD Moore

Back cover image courtesy of Jimmy Mitchell

Select interior images courtesy of Jimmy Mitchell, Eyal Warshvsky, Howie Rowling, and Preston Goldfarb

I want to dedicate my book to my parents, Isadore and Fannye Goldfarb, who taught me to always plant my feet firmly on the ground, know who I am, where I came from, and I will always find my way. I also dedicate this book, most importantly, to my beautiful wife, Marie; my son, Sean; his wife, Samantha; my grandson, Otis Wolf; granddaughter, Fiona Jade; daughter, Aly; and her husband, Jon. To my brother, Morton, and his family, who have also stood by me and helped guide me on my wonderful journey.

Contents

Preface..1

Chapter 1: Coaching Philosophy 5

Chapter 2: Coaching Tactics 11

Chapter 3: Beginnings 22

Chapter 4: Basketball...31

Chapter 5: Moving Up 42

Chapter 6: Military...48

Chapter 7: Finding Love...57

Chapter 8: CIA...65

Chapter 9: Hobbies 72

Chapter 10: BSC Beginnings..82

Chapter 11: More Building..89

Chapter 12: Building a Dynasty 97

Chapter 13: The NCAA Years 112

Chapter 14: Shift to Division III 123

Chapter 15: The Olympics Come to Legion Field................136

Chapter 16: Birmingham Grasshoppers.................................143

Chapter 17: Preston Goldfarb Field..152

Chapter 18: Soccer Camps...159

Chapter 19: The Next Generation 173

Chapter 20: Very Good Dogs...183

Chapter 21: Halls of Fame Times Three 190

Chapter 22: Maccabiah Beginnings...196

Chapter 23: Maccabiah Gold—Part 1 203

Chapter 24: Maccabiah Gold—Part 2 216

Chapter 25: How I Coached the Game 231

Year-by-Year Records..247

Pictures 251

Preface

M Y FIRST CONTACT WITH PRESTON GOLDFARB WAS BACK IN JUNE of 1996. I worked for a newspaper in Talladega, Alabama, and was getting ready to cover the Summer Olympics. Atlanta was the hub, but Birmingham was the home of several men's and women's soccer matches, which would be played at Legion Field. I didn't know the coach personally, but I knew that as far as soccer sources go, he was one of the best I could ever hope to find.

Not only was he well into his Hall of Fame career as head coach of the Birmingham-Southern College (BSC) men's soccer team, but he had been one of the leading patrons in convincing Olympic organizers to let Birmingham be part of the Games. He also coached Birmingham's United States Interregional Soccer League club, the Grasshoppers, and I had spent many an afternoon on the BSC campus watching that team play.

Soccer had been a passion of mine for years, and having a local team to support helped fuel that passion. But this call was more about the business of soccer instead of the pleasure of watching it. And if you wanted to talk intelligently about "The Beautiful Game," he could talk for hours and tell you everything you needed to know. His philosophy is best summed up in a speech he gave during his induction into the Jewish Sports Heritage Hall of Fame in 2018:

> *I always tried to build my programs like a professional team by the way we trained, played, dressed, and traveled. We succeeded way beyond my dreams. Our programs were always based on honor, loyalty, integrity, and commitment. We had three principles that defined our program, and they were family was always first, followed by education, and then soccer. We believed that the game of soccer is based on finding a rhythm to create a flow with great balance by playing possession soccer with the ball on the ground, as it is round and doesn't have wings, so it shouldn't fly. Our philosophy or system of buying in was to play simple, like a peanut butter and jelly sandwich on white bread with a glass of milk and not fancy like caviar and champagne. Training and repetition of our philosophy*

were the keys to our success. I know I wasn't the easiest coach to play for because I always demanded perfection each and every day, knowing perfection is never attainable but the effort of striving for perfection was. It was always about the players and the relationships built over the years of coaching, which afforded me the distinct opportunity to live and love the game.

The key to his team's success was simplicity. The key to his success in life, however, goes far beyond the simplicity of "peanut butter and jelly sandwich on white bread with a glass of milk." As much as I'll always respect him for what he has accomplished in soccer, what he's accomplished as a man is even more impressive. Think Walter Mitty; only instead of imagining himself leading a life of adventure, Coach Goldfarb actually went out and did it.

One of roughly six thousand Jews growing up in Birmingham during the dawn of the civil rights era, he overcame anti-Semitism to excel as a student, an athlete, and ultimately a teacher.

Despite being small in stature, he received a basketball scholarship from the University of Oklahoma. Injuries ended his college basketball career before it ever started, but it merely led him to other paths—paths that took him to law school, the army, photography, and even a brush with the Central Intelligence Agency.

Sure, hyperbole and fantasy make for a great story, but dreams that become reality make a much better one.

When Coach Goldfarb decided to write this book and allow me to be a small part of it, I was excited because of the soccer angle. Being able to bend the ear of one of its most successful coaches was a real honor. But then when he shared his incredible life experiences, I realized he has so much more to tell and that I, in turn, had so much more to learn. Bottom line, if you're a soccer fan you're going to love what you're about to read. But this is for anyone who has endured tragedy and triumph and faced obstacles and overcome them. This is Preston Goldfarb's story, and now it's time for me to step back and let him tell it.

—Scott Adamson

Chapter 1:
Coaching Philosophy

Basketball is my love because I grew up playing it, and in junior high I had what I think was my best coach, bar none. His name was Carl Roberts, and he was the meanest person I ever played for. He was brutal, but we had unbelievable teams. His worst season was my ninth-grade year when we finished 23–6. We averaged over one hundred points a game, and we were "run and gun." We used the old "Auburn Shuffle" that Coach Joel Eaves started when he was there, and it was the beginning of the motion offense that you see today. But it was all about understanding it. If you forgot where you were supposed to go after a certain pass or a certain move, Coach Roberts would hit you with his whistle lanyard or kick a ball at your stomach. I mean, back then you'd get paddled and all that kind of stuff.

I remember during a time-out, we were sitting on the floor and one of my teammates asked for a towel and Coach Roberts whacked him across the face with the back of his hand and said, "Don't you ever talk while I'm talking!" This was how he was, and you understood that. He got so angry one time during a junior high home game that he went into a rage. He was sitting in a chair on the bench and reared his head back and hit it so hard against the wall he actually knocked himself out. But he could've been a great college coach. He was the best coach I ever played for, and I really modeled a lot of how I coached after him because he was so tough. Now, I didn't do all that other mean stuff that he did, but he instilled in me that you have to work hard to get what you want.

In ninth grade during study hall, I would always play basketball with other people in the class and I got tripped and fell on my wrist. I knew immediately it was broken—I couldn't even pick up a piece of paper with that hand. I hated to go see him and tell him what had happened (my last class was art), but I did. And he told me he'd go talk to my teacher. Meanwhile, he instructed me to keep my hand in a bucket of ice. This happened right before the county tournament, and he said, "I'll tape it up, and you're going to practice." I said, "Sure." My right hand, which was my shooting hand, was numb. But he taped it up, and I went out to practice. Since I didn't have any feeling in it, I'd forgotten about the injury. I got the ball passed to me; it hurt like hell, and my hand broke in three places. So I went to the doctor that night, and he put me in a cast. I had to go back to school and tell Coach Roberts I couldn't play. He didn't speak to me for the longest time. He blamed me for losing the county tournament and said, "You could've played!" But that injury is how I learned to shoot with my left hand.

The bottom line is that Coach Roberts instilled in me the idea that practice was the most important thing. The games don't make you better, it's the practices that make you better. So I modeled that theory myself, in that I loved training. It's not necessarily the games I miss; I miss the practice field. I love teaching the game. Not that my way is the right way, but it's the way I believe in. As I've told people before, basketball was where my heart was until I went to Germany in 1972 and discovered soccer. That was life changing for me.

Soccer gets in your blood, and I think the reason I loved it was that it was very similar technically to basketball, which I knew really well. I could relate soccer tactics to a press, counterattacking like a fast break, and you could develop your system based on that. But I liked the fact that anyone could play the game regardless of their size. It's the only sport I knew where you could put twenty-two people on the field and all twenty-two people are involved in the game. It's not where you play for five seconds and then rest for thirty-five seconds. In football, over a sixty-minute game, the actual amount of action is a little less than fifteen minutes, but soccer is nonstop. There are no time-outs in soccer, so you can't call your team over and make changes. You get fifteen minutes at halftime to make all the changes you need to make during a game.

That's why I loved it because it put an emphasis on teaching the game in training so you could be productive on the weekend for your game. Coaches in other sports have such a big control during the game whether it's baseball, basketball, football, or whatever it is. You have time-outs, you have innings, you have breaks at quarters, and you can make adjustments as the game is going on. In soccer, you can't. You make those adjustments in training, and you tweak them a little bit at halftime to counter what the other team is doing. I had a philosophy that we are going to play our game regardless of what the other team does. In order for them to beat us, they're going to have to play equal to us or better than us, but we're not going to develop our system every week based on what the other team does. We're going to do our system, and we're going to do it as proficiently as we can, making the other team have to rise to our level.

A coach can overcoach, meaning you can change things every week to accommodate what the other team does, but what you do is you wind up not accommodating your own team. You develop your system based on your players; you don't make your players play a certain system. You develop how your players are going to play by how good they are at doing what you think they should be able to do. I always felt like I wanted to create the perfect game. And knowing that perfection was never possible, the act of trying to be as perfect as possible allows you to do your best. That's what we did. By trying to be perfect, we tried to work hard in training to develop that perfection. We knew it was unattainable, but the effort of striving for perfection was attainable. We felt like if you started at 100 percent, you're probably going to attain 80 percent, which is effective. But if you start at 80 percent, you're barely going to get to 60 percent. And that is not acceptable. That's how we developed our system over the years. So we started at 100 percent, knowing that we could get 80 percent for ninety minutes of the game, and that's what you want out of that.

I remember, in my last years of coaching at Birmingham-Southern, having a great conversation with the coach at Washington University, Joe Clark, who is a dear friend. He coached at Saint Louis University for years, and they would go to the NCAA tournament all the time and make it to the semifinals quite frequently, and even the finals. But he went one or two years where they didn't do so well, so he got fired. And he was there for a long time. He went to Washington University where he's done an unbelievable job with the D3 program. We had a long conversation one time, and he said, "You know, we get our pick of kids here. We have to turn away so many kids who want to play because they can't get in. And I don't have to recruit; the school recruits for me. But I get these kids, and they have no idea how to think." So we had that long conversation about thinking, and we were on the same page about that when I told him my thoughts. Kids today are not taught how to think on the field. Until that happens with the youth and until the best athletes start playing soccer, or at least the ones willing to think for the betterment of their team, we're not going to do anything internationally, in my opinion. You can teach your kid technical things, but getting them to think is a whole different ball game. You have to have that and ultimately a professional league with promotion/relegation. Until those things happen, we're never going to improve. It just becomes stagnant.

Chapter 2:

Coaching Tactics

WHEN I STARTED WITH SOCCER BACK IN THE EARLY 1970S, I DIDN'T really know a whole lot about the game. All I did was apply what I thought would be appropriate to the game based on my background in basketball; I felt like soccer was very akin to basketball, in that the only difference being that in basketball you play with your hands and in soccer you play with your feet. But all the tactics were very similar from offensive movement off the ball to defensive pressure. So I tried to adapt that in setting up systems of play. And of course I read a lot and tried to figure out what was best for the kind of players we had. It was a very evolving time for me, and to learn it better, I felt I needed to go play the game. I went into it mentally for about eight years but then decided to play so I'd have firsthand knowledge of the game as a player as well. That way I can relate to the players what I was trying to do as a coach.

It all started with coaching my brother's youngest son in youth soccer. At that time they were playing in the YMCA league, which was really the only league around in the mid-1970s. Prior to that I'd coached at Birmingham University School (now the Altamont School) and started the soccer program there. I carried that experience into coaching my nephew's young team and wanted to pull it away from the YMCA and into a different league. That led to the Mid-State Soccer League, which was the largest youth organization in the state at that time. We had a team called BEST (Birmingham East Soccer Team), Birmingham United, and a couple of other good teams. We had our own championships and state championships within, and it worked out well. And then I moved on to what was known as Independent Soccer Club Strikers of Birmingham, and there were some players on that team that actually came to play for me at the college, which was great. David Kearney is one who comes to mind, as well as John Michael Bodnar—both were actually on the first club team that we formed. So all this was before I started with Birmingham-Southern, and that's where I started to learn tactics. Besides reading and watching *Soccer Made in Germany* on the old PBS channel every Sunday, trying to just soak up as much as I could from watching, I learned all that I could. And once I started my licensing training in Germany, going once or twice a year to learn not only tactics but training too, what I found was I was really deficient in my learning knowledge of the game. So I decided to keep that going for another six or seven years until I finally got my license. And what I came up with, really, were two things. One is the thing that you'll hear me say numerous times, which is what I call "simple soccer"—a peanut butter and jelly sandwich on white bread with a glass of milk, not caviar and champagne. Simple, not fancy, was the basis of the way I taught because I wanted the game to be simple, not complicated. A lot of times coaches impart a lot of different things to their teams that are complicated, and the kids have a difficult time figuring things out. Kids have to be able to think on the field, but if you give them too much to think about, then it becomes a real issue within the flow of the game.

A coach must also have the courage to create their own conditions. What I mean by that is understanding and developing a system that gears itself toward the players. A lot of times, coaches will put in a system with no real inkling as to what the players can or cannot perform within that system. So what you have to do is create your own conditions, and a coach must use repetition to replicate those conditions every day to become successful. That success is not measured by the scoreboard but rather by the conditions the coach had the courage to implement successfully in their team. All that is done during training, and you learn that soccer is a game of repetition.

It's not a natural game for Americans, in my opinion. It's not something that we all grew up with—now it is a bit—but before we were taught to use our hands for playing basketball, baseball, football, and games like that. And when it's not a natural game, we have to really understand the game itself and how to develop it. You don't impart your thoughts of how players have to fit into a system you've already created but rather how to develop a system that fits them best in order to be successful on the field. And I think that's really important in the rationale of playing simple soccer. If you complicate things and you want them to do things that they see on TV and all these different fancy moves and things like that, that won't make you successful. I would get very angry about that because juggling the ball down the field is not soccer. And the more times you touch the ball, the less chance you have of being successful with your next pass or your next movement because every touch gives your opponent a chance to recover and get behind the ball to defend against you. So in training all our drills were based on three touches or less. If you took more than three touches, the ball went over to the other side, whatever drill we were doing.

And I used that drill all the time. I would do three touches, then two touches, and then we'd play a one-touch game in a very confined space where we'd get inside the 18-yard box and play 10-on-10 one touch. It's kind of chaotic in there, but it forced them to have to find their opponent in a very congested area. We did that quite a lot during my time of coaching, and it was a great way of teaching tactics. Sometimes we'd have two goalkeepers and play on a fifty by fifty grid, sometimes even smaller, and we'd play 10 versus 10. Every time you played a ball, you had to move, and if you didn't move or you put more than two touches on the ball, it went over to the other side. And the ball had to be played on the ground. The only time the ball could get in the air is if you got it to the corner on the ground, then a person could cross the ball. The old English style, going back years, was kick and run—just kick the ball and run after it. The game today has changed into more of a possession game and game of tactics, and the ball should be on the ground. That was always my philosophy. Even when I didn't know a whole lot, I knew that the ball was round and that the best way to move the ball is on the ground. And I credit a lot of that to my training in Germany. I got my license in 1991 but continued going there until 1997 to learn more from a lot of coaches, talking to them, learning what their philosophy was, going to their training, and watching their training sessions.

Every player is different, and you have to base what you know on what's best for your team to be successful, not on what you think is right. You can't teach them to do it one way every single time. As a coach, you have to learn the game and you have to study the game. And you have to be able to develop a system that fits your players both in training and on tactics during the game.

One reason I love soccer is there are no time-outs. So what you do in training is what you have to do in the game. My comparison is a professor in college or a teacher in high school or grammar school who teaches for a whole week on a subject. And then at the end of the week, you have an exam to measure if the teacher has taught you properly and you've learned what was taught. It's the same thing in soccer. You teach during training, and then the game is the exam. You watch the game, and during that game, you see if you did the right things in training to prepare them. And I can unequivocally tell you that I have never scouted another team, ever. I felt like I only had to scout my team. And if I prepared my team properly to do the things that we think will be successful, it doesn't matter what the other team does. If we play at our level, doing the things we're taught, the other team will have to either play equal to us or better than us to win the game. If you're scouting to change your philosophy, that's not the right approach, in my opinion. Others see it differently, of course. They all scout teams, and I know we were scouted a lot of times. But I felt like if I did my job of teaching the players in training, how we're going to apply what we've learned through repetition, over and over and over again, was the key. You don't go onto a basketball court and just automatically play, you do drills over and over and over again. You shoot layups, and you shoot free throws, over and over and over again. You do your plays over and over and over again. It's the repetition that's important.

Unfortunately, I had some players who didn't like that and would voice their opinion that they wanted to do a lot of different drills during training. It wasn't fun to do the same drill over and over and over. But I said the game is not about being fun in training but the game is about working hard in training and becoming proficient in what we're trying to teach so the game becomes a simple game for us. They want that part to be fun, but that's the problem. Some people today don't want to work hard to get better and do the repetition.

To start every practice, we usually did a few drills the same way every single day. We started our training session with warm-up, and I would train for ninety minutes, religiously. I felt like if you got your body in tune to training ninety minutes, then it'll be prepared for a game, which is also ninety minutes. I wanted our metabolism to be the same in training as it was in a game. So we'd spend the first twenty minutes warming up, but the warm-up was not as normal.

We would do a drill called 5 versus 2 for ten minutes or one touch on a seven by seven or eight by eight small grid. We'd fit players around the perimeter to the middle as defenders and play one touch, and after ten minutes, we'd stop and start our stretching exercises. I always did ballistic exercises later in my career, but earlier the thing was static stretching before you did anything.

As time has evolved and so has learning, you find that stretching before warming up is like taking a branch of a tree. If you put it in your hand and hold it for a while, it warms up and then it just bends. But if you take it and bend it immediately, it cracks. So you want your muscles to be warmed up, and after ballistic stretching—which is movement stretching across the field and back for five minutes—we'd come back and play for another five minutes, then another five to ten minutes of ballistic stretching again. And then we'd go into something that I called "The Joker," which is a continuation of the warm-up for another ten to fifteen minutes. And that was 10 versus 10 plus one. The plus one was the Joker, and that person only played on the attacking team, so the attacking team was 11 versus 10. We'd put a three touch or two touch limit on it and play on a half field. Most of the time, we'd reduce the size of the field to usually fifty or sixty yards, or something like that. We would play that and change the Joker every so often so that person was in the middle. Sometimes we played twenty minutes, and we would do our last set of ballistic stretching. Then we were ready to get into our game situation, which involved tactical drills. And we did all our preliminary drills during preseason—shooting, touch drills, and things like that. Once we're in the season, we'd have a lot of small-sided games, sometimes on a field of twenty by twenty-five. Our tactics were always geared to the way we play.

Back when I coached, most teams played with two strikers, so you had a sweeper and two marking backs and five midfielders. Then the game evolved to more complex systems of play, but the systems that we used were either the 3-5-2 or 4-5-1, based on what kind of players we had. If we didn't have the kind to make the 3-5-2 work, we would play in a 4-5-1 situation, which was a very defensive, counterattacking situation. A 3-5-2 is more of an offensive situation. The team I had at Birmingham-Southern in 1995 was basically a very attack-oriented team, so the 3-5-2 suited them well. And if we got a lead on a very good team, we would fall back into a 4-5-1 to play defense, hold our lead, and counterattack. But you had to have the players able to play those systems, and there are so many different systems out there. Coaches want to put in systems of play that they like, but sometimes it just doesn't fit the players.

You've got to be able to analyze your players and make sure you give them the best chance for success by putting them in a system that works for them, not a system you want to play necessarily.

The point I'm trying to make is that the coach must be able to analyze his or her players and determine what's best for them to give them the skills that they need in order to be successful in the game. To me that's more important than a coach trying to show them how much he knows or thinks he knows about the game. Sometimes you go out and watch these games during their training and often see tremendous number of cones on the field. And you know that when you do things like that, it's just trying to impress someone and make them think you know what you're doing when in essence you really don't know. I was not a big proponent of that.

Everything that we did was pointed toward the game, the way we would play and the drills that we would do, and we would go over and over and over again. That, I think, is what was really important. You've got to have the courage to create your own conditions that give your team the best chance to succeed. And I felt like that was the easiest way to go about things. And that's been my philosophy the whole time—play simple. The game is a simple game, and it's the coaches who make it really, really complicated. And I think that the way we tried to do things was the right way, and it was way I was taught in Germany. So my philosophies about tactics and how to play the game is based on my players, not on my thoughts, and a coach has to be able to understand what his players can and cannot do. You teach it and you teach it and you teach it, and you play it over and over and over again during training so it's not foreign to you once the game begins. By then you've seen it a thousand times in training, and when something happens, you know from the repetitive drills done in training you're always prepared for what you see during a game. You're never surprised, and you expect what is seen during the course of the game.

Chapter 3:
Beginnings

I WAS INDUCTED INTO THE JEWISH SPORTS HERITAGE HALL OF FAME back in 2018, and part of that ceremony involved making an acceptance speech. I had a lot to say and many people to thank, but one main point I wanted to make was this: Most athletes use sports as a way out; I used it as a way in.

That requires an explanation, of course, and I'll get to that. Before I do, though, I hope you might indulge me as I give you some background about who I am and how my journey began.

My father, Isadore Goldfarb, was born in Birmingham, and his parents lived in Birmingham as well. His mom died very young, and his dad passed a few years after that. My dad's father came over from Germany. We never really understood all the details of that, but I know we lost some people on his side in the Holocaust.

My mom's parents were from Ukraine; then they came to the United States and settled in Rome, Georgia. That's where my mom, Fannye Shapiro, was born, but when she was a young child, they all moved to Birmingham. She met my dad in Birmingham, and they got married and made the city their home—and ultimately, the home of my brother and me. I remember my father telling me stories about his family not having food on the table, so he would go out and sell hot tamales to try and buy a loaf of bread just so they would have something to eat—they were that poor. My mother's father was a peddler, and he would get in his car and go peddle his merchandise on the roads of Birmingham.

Living through all that I think really resulted in a great work ethic for my mom and dad, and when they got married, they had a grocery store on the northside of Birmingham that was actually built on the site of the city's first jail. It was a place called Enon Ridge, and it's part of the Birmingham Civil Rights Heritage Trail. If you study some history of Birmingham, you'll learn it was one of the first prime residential neighborhoods for African Americans in the first half of the twentieth century. As for my family (my older brother, Dr. Morton Goldfarb, was born in 1938), they lived in the Norwood community on Huntsville Road. But in 1947 when I was born, my father bought his uncle's department store in Birmingham; it was called the Fair Department Store. They had the department store from 1947 until my dad retired in 1973. And he lived a year and a half after retiring and then passed away in his sleep from a massive heart attack. Even though my mom and dad grew up poor, my dad did really well with the department store, enough to help us move to Mountain Brook. My first-grade year, I went to MacArthur School for half the year (it was located right down the street from my home on Huntsville Road). Then in 1954, we moved to the Crestline area, and I went to the Crestline Elementary School and Mountain Brook Junior High for seventh, eighth, and ninth grades, before I went on to Shades Valley High School. There was no Mountain Brook High School at that time.

My folks were hard workers; they both worked together at the store. They had one car, and my mom would take my dad to work in the morning, then come home and make dinner, and then leave it on the stove so they could heat it up when they both got home from work. My dad was a gambler; he did that on the side. He was a bookie, and honestly I have very fond memories of that because there were a lot of stories there.

He couldn't serve in the military due to his poor eyesight, but he was chairman of the local North Birmingham and surrounding areas draft board under five presidents, starting with his appointment by

Dwight Eisenhower in 1959, then John Kennedy, Lyndon Johnson, Richard Nixon, and finally Gerald Ford. His tenure lasted from 1959 until his death in 1975. He also received commendation letters from all of them as well.

Overall I've always thought I had an idyllic life. I couldn't have had a better childhood, and even though my brother was nine years older than me, we were very close. Of course because of the age difference, he was already out of the house when I was in high school. In fact, when I was in fourth grade, he was in the army.

Before joining he went to Birmingham-Southern and basically flunked because he was in love and that commanded most of his attention. So he joined the army, but then after he got out, he came back and finished school at Birmingham-Southern, ending up making the dean's list, and got married when he was nineteen. He and his wife lived in our house for about a year until they could stand on their feet, but then he went on and finished school and became a very highly rated ear, nose, and throat and plastic surgeon in Birmingham. It was another case of the work ethic in our family. He started something and finished it.

Again, I couldn't have asked for a better childhood—it was a special time back then for us. But as you might imagine in Birmingham, Alabama, in the 1950s, there were a lot of issues with religion and race. I was a Jewish kid in a Jewish family, and during my whole time as a grammar school and high school student I went to segregated schools. We had no Black students at all, and it wasn't until about 1967 the schools became integrated in Birmingham. I graduated in 1966, so I missed all that. But my experience was a lot different. Because of their work at the store, my parents hired a maid—Edwina Chapman. She was a Black woman who basically raised me, and I wouldn't trade that for anything. Beyond that, I'd say 99 percent of the clientele at our store—where I worked every summer—was Black, so we had a great relationship with African Americans. I think it was a situation where we understood what they were going through and they understood what we were going through, so there was a bond there. And the big thing, I think, is that my parents were wonderful. Our parents always had a Sunday dinner with our family that my brother and I continue to this day with our families, which is what they always taught us about the family being the most important part of our lives. They raised my brother and me the right way and taught us to be the best people we could possibly be. I think maybe in your childhood you get shielded from a lot of the bad things going on around you, but I distinctly remember encountering my first brush with anti-Semitism in grammar school. We didn't know it when we moved to Mountain Brook, but it was very elitist and very anti-Semitic at the time. On

April 28, 1958, fifty-four sticks of dynamite were placed outside Temple Beth-El, Birmingham's conservative synagogue, in a bombing attempt. According to police reports, the burning fuses were doused by heavy rainfall, preventing the dynamite from exploding. Although the crime was never solved, police considered Bobby Frank Cherry, later convicted of bombing the 16th Street Baptist Church, to be a suspect. The 16th Street Baptist Church bombing, killing four little girls, was on September 15, 1963.

I can still remember getting phone calls in the middle of the night from the KKK, telling us they were going to burn crosses in our yard if we didn't move away. They said Jews were not welcome in our state. I also have vivid memories of my father's store being broken into many times, and we were not sure if it was just vandalism or the KKK at work again, trying to hurt our family any way they could.

Birmingham had two main country clubs, the Birmingham Country Club and Mountain Brook Country Club. Not only were no Jews allowed to belong but you couldn't even go there as a guest or anything. I mean, I'm not kidding when I say they just simply wouldn't let you in. I knew that, but in grammar school, I had some friends who were not Jewish and there was never a problem. Then there were also kids I knew who were always calling me all kinds of bad names and saying horrible things like I killed Christ and stuff like that. You took what you could take but having said that, I got in a lot of fights in grammar school. And that's OK. I guess I understood the words and taunts were things that I was just going to have to deal with. But my first really bad encounter, or the thing that really stuck with me the most, was in junior high school.

In the seventh grade, I'd gotten a bicycle for my bar mitzvah. When a Jewish person turns thirteen, they become a man in the Jewish religion. My rabbi was Seymour Atlas (he published a book called *The Rabbi With the Southern Twang: True Stories From a Life of Leadership Within the Orthodox Jewish Congregations of the South*, and he became our rabbi after serving as rabbi at Agudath Israel Synagogue. Agudath Israel came to national attention in the wake of the Montgomery Bus Boycott of 1955. At that time Rabbi Atlas had been serving at Agudath Israel for almost ten years. A southerner (from Greenville, Mississippi), he was the eighth generation of a line of rabbis and had become friends with Martin Luther King Jr., tutoring him in Hebrew and speaking at his Dexter Avenue church. As a result of his friendship with King, Rabbi Atlas became involved in the civil rights movement and known for his liberal sermons, for also appearing on local television and radio stations with King, where he would discuss civil rights and issues, including desegregation and the boycott. Rabbi Atlas was subsequently fired because of his relationship with King, and that was how we were fortunate to get him as our rabbi at Knesseth Israel Synagogue.

You go through a ceremony, you read from the Torah (the five books of Moses), you make a speech, and you have it all in the synagogue. Well, that bicycle was a gift, and I rode it to school one day, which was just down the street from where we lived. This guy stole it from me and not just because he wanted a bike—he told me the reason he stole it was because I was a Jew. I finally got it back, but right after it happened, I ran home crying and was totally devastated. I'd heard words from people like that before and dealt with it, but I'd never seen anybody take something from someone just because of their religion.

But that turned out to be pivotal in my life because that's when I decided I was going to use that kind of attitude to my advantage. And what I mean by that is that I wanted to make people understand that just because we were Jewish didn't mean we were bad—we weren't bad. And it wasn't long before I decided the way to do that was through athletics.

While most people use athletics as a way out—a way out of an environment, a way out of poverty, or just a way to make themselves known and make money—I wanted to use it as a way in. It was a way to be accepted for who I was as an athlete—not because of my religion or anything else but just because of athletics. I'd use that to propel me and make me a better person. I wanted to make people appreciate things about me, and I felt if they did that, they would understand me better as a person.

Who knew I'd be revisiting that theme again in a speech almost sixty years later?

Chapter 4:

Basketball

ALTHOUGH SOCCER IS WHAT I'M MOST ASSOCIATED WITH, IT wasn't something that was part of my early life at all. Instead, I played basketball—that was my sport. We didn't have soccer back then, or I guess it's more accurate to say I just didn't know anything about it. And really, I didn't learn how to play basketball until I was ten years old and didn't know anything about athletics in general. But the memory that's still so vivid in my mind is the one where I was standing outside in our front yard, watching a couple of kids playing basketball. Our neighbor across the street had a basket, and that's where the kids were playing. I went over there and watched them and thought they were pretty good. Of course I tried to play myself, but I didn't know anything about the game at all—I was double dribbling, and they had to tell me to do this and not to do that and basically explain all the rules to me. So my dad came up to me and said, "I'm going to enroll you in biddy basketball." (Biddy basketball was formed in 1951 and designed to teach boys and girls basketball skills and fundamentals while gearing the goals and balls to their heights). I told my dad I didn't know what that is, didn't know how to play, and didn't want to embarrass myself. But lo and behold, I did get involved in biddy basketball in 1957.

The Jewish Community Center had just opened, and as a child I had learned how to swim at the old YMHA downtown, which is right across the street from the Alabama Power building. That was a place for Jewish people to go. It was similar to the YMCA—it was the Young Men's Hebrew Association. In 1957 they moved to Montclair Road and had a biddy basketball program. The coach, Ralph Thomas, who taught me how to swim was the overall coach of all the sports at the YMHA. He's one of the greatest people I've ever known. I had a special relationship with Coach Thomas, and he was a great athlete in his own right. He graduated from Samford University (or Howard College as it was known back then), but he worked at the Jewish Community Center until he retired. I would go there early in the morning in the summer when I was a kid before I started working. They would open up at 8:00 a.m., and I would get there then and not come home until 9:00 p.m. And as I got more interested in basketball, I developed some heroes. When it comes to my idols, there were really two. One was Oscar Robertson from the Cincinnati Royals, and my biggest was Bob Cousy.

A friend of my father knew Cousy and got him to send a picture of himself that was autographed to me, and I still have that. I loved Cousy because he wasn't big. I just fell in love with him, and through him I also fell in love with the Boston Celtics. Both he and Robertson were both point guards. Robertson was six feet five, but Cousy was barely six feet tall. I tried to model myself after how they played, even down to wearing their numbers when I could. I liked the way they played, but I liked the way they conducted themselves also.

I did more than just play basketball, though. I'd also swim and play baseball and tried to participate in whatever sport was going on. When I was ten, I also started playing handball and fell in love with it. To this day I still believe that handball really helped my abilities as a basketball player more than anything, especially in terms of coordination, quickness, and vision. I got to play all over the region, winning a lot of tournaments, both as a singles player and as a doubles player with my good friend, Phil Teninbaum. I also won the handball championship at the University of Oklahoma when I was a freshman. Really, handball is still the one sport I miss more than anything from a participation standpoint. But basketball became the thing that I truly fell for and played year-round.

We didn't have a basket in our yard, but the neighbors I mentioned earlier did. So the place I first went to and saw the other kids playing became my training ground. My very best friend growing up was Arnold Simon, who lived two houses down from us, and he and I would play basketball every day and night that we could. We would play whatever sport was in season, including playing Wiffle ball in my backyard. We had teams, and every Saturday in the summer, we played, rain or shine. It was the best of times growing up and always playing outside. We have remained best friends to this day, and having him just two houses down made it very easy for us to play and get better at basketball. I truly believe he was very important in my becoming a better basketball player, because we always played together. He didn't play in junior high or high school but was always there to help me get better. They'd even leave the lights on for me just so I could go over there and shoot after it got dark. Ultimately, that helped give me the opportunity to play in junior high and high school and an opportunity to play in college. It was such a great way to get people to understand me as a person as opposed to criticizing me for my religion because they didn't know me. And my parents would always go wherever I went to play, so they were there to support me, which meant a lot to me. Now, I didn't really experience anti-Semitic slurs at the junior high level, but I definitely had to deal with it in high school once I got to Shades Valley. We'd go play games out in Jefferson County, places like Mortimer Jordan, and I distinctly remember one incident where I dove for a ball on the ground—the stands back then were right down on the court and basically just chairs. This one guy was sitting on the front row, and as I was going for the loose ball, he yelled at me, "Crawl, Jew, crawl!" That really hit me pretty hard. I got up, picked up the ball, and threw it right in his face. And I got escorted out of the gym, obviously. But I remember that like it was yesterday.

I did encounter an issue on my own team in high school with a player who went to junior high school with me. We played together there and then got to high school where we were on the B team together. Actually there were five of us who played together on that team, and all got called up to the varsity as tenth graders. But our junior year that one player—I don't want to use his name—wasn't quite good enough to move up, so he stayed on the B team and didn't get back to varsity until his senior year. But his dad was a big booster, so you probably know where this story is heading. Before I get into that, though, I should tell you about Bill Corr—he and I grew up together and became best friends, and we are still best friends to this day. When President Barack Obama was in office,

Bill went on to serve as deputy secretary under Health and Human Services Secretary Kathleen Sebelius until she left office. But growing up, we were very close and really good players. Even our coach, Jim Tolson, touted Bill and me as the two best guards in the state, and we were being promoted that way. And we were dedicated to the game. Between my sophomore and junior year, Bill and I both went to France and we studied at a university over there for twelve weeks and toured around. But we took our leg weights, hand weights, jump rope, and basketball with us. We practiced over there every day ourselves. A lot of the other guys on our high school team played other sports, but Bill and I didn't. We concentrated strictly on basketball. We always had our pregame meals at each other's home, with our mom's cooking steak and baked potatoes for us. Sometimes, we would go to a restaurant in Mountain Brook village called the Buttery (no longer there) and get a steak, baked potato, and salad for $1.50!

Well, we used to shoot free throws together on the court and talk about different things strategywise and just work out together quite a bit. Before specific games we'd discuss how we were going to address the press, deal with matchups, and so forth. And then one day, I'm called into the coach's office along with Bill and we're told that we can't work out like that anymore and that we have to be a basket apart when we're shooting. I don't think we understood what was going on—I know I didn't. I was being touted as an all-state player at the time and being recruited by colleges. But that wasn't the worst part because after that meeting—and during my senior year when I was expected to be one of the top performers on our team—I was demoted to third string for no apparent reason. I wasn't even on the court; I had to sit in the bleachers during practice. I came home and told my father and my mom what had happened, and I was in tears. I just said, "I'm going to quit. I'm not going to be embarrassed like that and have to sit in the bleachers during practice." I got on the phone with Bill and told him I was quitting, and he tried to talk me out of it. But then my dad came over and told me that I wasn't quitting. We went back and forth with the "Yes, I am" and "No, you're not" until he won the argument. And I'll remember this until the day I die. He said, "If you're better than he is, it'll come out in the end." I asked him, "How can it come out in the end if I can't even get on the court?" He said, "You have to trust me. If you sit on the bench, then you need to be the best bench-sitter there is. You support your teammates and you sit there. You don't pout, you applaud your teammates, and you move on." He reinforced not quitting by telling me, "Once you start quitting, it becomes easier each time you are faced with adversity." What he also told me I have carried with me my entire life and that was, "Always plant your feet firmly on the ground, know who you are, where you came from, and you will always find your way"! How true that was then, and how true it remains today in my life.

During our run to get to the state tournament, we played in the regional tournament and won. So we qualified for the state tournament, and as usual I didn't start either game. But during the finals to make it to the state, we were losing early in the game. I was sent in, and we went on a great run to win the game. My father's words resonated in my head as I made the All-Tournament without starting either game, "If you are better than he is, it will come out in the end." Like he said, it would come out in the end, and I did win my starting job back at the state tournament. But a lot happened leading up to that.

My father was very vocal in the stands, but it was always all positive. He was rooting for everybody, not just me, but he was loud and I could hear him. We were playing a game at Berry High School before the state tournament back in 1966, and what stood out was that I didn't hear him during the course of the game, which we won. That just didn't seem right. Bill and I would always go out and get a hamburger after a game, but this time I knew something was wrong since my dad wasn't cheering us on. So instead of getting together with Bill and doing our postgame ritual, I felt like I needed to go home. When I got there, I saw an ambulance at my house—my dad had suffered a massive heart attack. They rushed him to the hospital, and by the time they got there, he was basically dead. But my brother was a resident at the time and called in one of the most noted heart guys in the world, Tinsley R. Harrison, and he came out and made a couple of adjustments to my dad's medicine. That saved his life, and he went on to live nine more years. Obviously he couldn't follow the team to the state tournament, and in my situation I guessed I wasn't going to play anyway, even though I had been considered an MVP candidate up until I was benched. But what happened when we went to state is my dad sent my brother to write down everything that was going on so he could keep up. The games weren't on the radio, so there was no other way he could find out. We played Sydney Lanier High School out of Montgomery, and their smallest guy was six feet one. They had one guy who went on to play for Alabama and two guys who went on to play for Auburn, so they were a very good team. Our number one center, who was six feet one, was sick and didn't play, and his replacement was 0-for-9 from the free-throw line.

When they announced the starting lineup for us, they announced the other player who had been starting ahead of me.

But Coach Tolson needed me in this game and decided I'd get the start, so he went over and told the PA announcer and scorekeeper there had been a change in the starting lineup. We lost that game by two points, but my brother got to record what I had done and report back to my dad. Even though it wasn't until that last game I won my job back, I got to go back and tell my dad, "You were right. If I was good enough and better than him, it'd come out in the end. And it did."

I had an inkling of what was going on as far as me being benched, but I wasn't 100 percent sure until a few years later. In 1971 or 1972, Tolson went to Livingston University, which is now West Alabama. He called me and asked if I wanted to go there and be his assistant.

So my dad and I drove down there, and when we got there, I knew pretty quickly it just wasn't really where I wanted to be. But I wanted to go through with the interview and just see what he had to say. So we finished talking about the job, and finally I said, "Coach, there's a question that I really want to ask you. Why was I benched as a senior back in 1966? And why was I not even second team but demoted to the third team?"

He told me he felt badly about what happened but he had pressure from the father of the player who replaced me. The father told him, "You shouldn't play a Jew over someone from your own religion," and then told him if he did that he was going to stop the booster money from coming in and get him fired. I don't know what I expected my reaction to be once I learned the truth, but I remember saying, "Coach, I respect you less now than I did then for listening to people like that." I left, and that was it. But at least I found out what happened and why. It was just a very tough time for me to have to go through that period during my senior year.

Chapter 5:
Moving Up

AS A SENIOR IN HIGH SCHOOL, YOU BEGIN THINKING ABOUT COL-
lege, and that was the year that my basketball recruitment
actually started. An interesting fact about that is in my senior year,
I had messed up my ankle really badly, and I knew if I didn't play,
I wouldn't have a chance of doing anything as far as getting looks
from college programs. In fact, at one point I was in a cast and was
supposed to stay in one much longer that I did. So how did I con-
vince my doctor to remove it earlier? I didn't. This sounds really
strange, but I forged my doctor's signature and what the "note"
said was that I was OK and cleared to play basketball. I went into
the locker room, got the cast wet in the shower, and then cut it off.
After that I wrapped my ankle in an ACE bandage and told my
coach I was good to go and handed him the doctor's note. He said,
"I want to see you sprint" to make sure my ankle was healed, and I

sprinted away from him so he wouldn't be able to see the grimace on my face. The pain was unbelievable. But I learned to live with it, and I was able to get through my senior season. I knew that if I was ever going to play basketball in college, I certainly had to play my senior year, and that was something I was able to accomplish.

I've already explained some of the things that happened on and off the court that year, but as far as recruiting was concerned, it picked up early in the season when I was playing really well. I was recruited by Troy, Livingston (now West Alabama), Howard College (now Samford), and Birmingham-Southern, and I even thought I had a chance to go to Alabama because Tolson had become Hayden Riley's assistant coach in basketball before moving on to Livingston. That didn't happen, but Tolson wrote a letter to Coach (Bob) Stevens at Oklahoma, and I got a shot to go there and play. What's funny about that situation, though, is that my dad and I got confused about the recruitment. He felt the best place for me to play would be Oklahoma State, where Hank Iba was the coach at the time. Iba is a member of the Basketball Hall of Fame and had led Oklahoma State to back-to-back national championships in the 1940s back when the school was known as Oklahoma A&M. He didn't play an up-tempo style but a slow-down type of game, which suited my style of play because it involved ball control and being able to pass the ball well.

But we got confused and instead of going to Stillwater, where Oklahoma State is located, we went to Norman and University of Oklahoma which was led by Coach Stevens. The freshman coach at the time was John MacLeod, who later became the Phoenix Suns coach and also coached at Notre Dame. He was a great guy, and I got to know a lot of great players on that team. One was Gar Heard, who was from LaGrange, Georgia, and ended up being drafted by the Chicago Bulls. He was Black, and it was the first time I ever played or went to school with a Black person. He was also a great guy—from the South like me—and then there was a fellow named Clifford Ray who went on to play for the Golden State Warriors. With players like that, I was on the bench, obviously, and during the first part of the training session of preseason practice with the freshman team, I got hurt again. They sent me to a clinic in Oklahoma City called the McBride Bone and Joint Clinic, and I was put in a cast and told that my ankle would never be the same. So knowing that my dreams of playing college basketball were over, I decided to come back home after the school year was out in 1967 and gave up competitive basketball. I loved Oklahoma. It was a great school, and I met a lot of nice friends there, but that was basically it for basketball for me as far as my playing career. I came home and I would play pick up ball at the Jewish Community Center, but even that ended badly. In 1974 while I was playing, some guy shoved me, and I fell and tore my ACL. That was back when they just took it out—they didn't repair it—so I don't have an ACL in my right knee. I don't know why, but somehow I always got injured. As far as what I wanted to do educationwise, I considered a few different things before I settled on becoming a coach.

Obviously with my brother being a doctor, I thought I wanted to do that, so my sophomore, junior, and part of my senior years in college I prepared for that by working in the operating room at Saint Vincent's Hospital. My brother got me a position there called an operating room technician, or ORT. There was a nun in charge of the operating room, Sister Michael Ann, and she was a wonderful person. She and I got along really well, and she really helped and encouraged me. I'd gotten to the point where I was basically a scrub nurse and getting called in to work a lot. I got to help with a lot of big-time doctors, including many whom I knew when I was growing up. They would take me over an intern—they would want me to help them instead—and that was kind of flattering. But in my senior year, I was getting calls to come in and work and sometimes I would go forty-eight hours without getting any sleep, and that made me realize this was not something that I really wanted to do. In addition, my grades weren't good enough to go forward with it because I kind of just fiddled around.

My dad always said that he wanted me to be involved in athletics, and I just thought, "I want to be a coach." So what I did was switch my major from biology to physical education, and I went to the University of Alabama at Birmingham (UAB) in 1967 and finished there with a degree in PE. I went on to get a master's at Montevallo in 1972 and started teaching and coaching at the old Birmingham University School. It was a private school, and in 1975, my last year of teaching there, it merged with Brook Hill, which was an all-girls school, and became the Altamont School. I taught biology, chemistry, and physiology and coached basketball and soccer. The guy who was the basketball coach—Werner Beiersdoerfer— was a great basketball coach and also an outstanding track coach. I went over to help him, and then when he left, I coached basketball and started the soccer program. I enjoyed coaching, and my dad came to everything I ever did even when I played in a men's softball league—softball used to be really big in Birmingham, and there were quite a few good, competitive teams in the area.

At the time I thought basketball would be what I wanted to coach, and I wanted to coach at the college level. However, I knew that not having been a college basketball player with a great track record behind me meant it would be a big mountain to climb if I was to be a college basketball coach. I just didn't think I had a chance with that.

But then I fell in love with soccer. In 1973 I went to Germany with my brother. At the time I was fluent in German, and he was not. He was looking to buy a German shepherd dog to start his breeding practice, so we went all over Germany looking for top German shepherds. While I was there, we would sit in bars and talk to people, and I would always watch what was on TV, which often happened to be soccer. The first time I saw it, I remember saying, "Golly, this looks a lot like basketball but played with your feet." All the tactics were the same; everything about the game was the same, but I didn't really know anything about it. That's when I started thinking, though, that I really liked the game a lot and I could do something with it. So that's how the soccer started, my leaving basketball to go into soccer as a coach. In the middle of all that, while I was teaching, I started law school at Birmingham School of Law at night in 1975. I went there thinking that's what I wanted to do, and as it turned out, it wasn't what I wanted to do at all. I finished school in 1978, and I was clerking for Chris and Taylor Law Firm and realized I didn't want to do law. So I started working at UAB Hospital in administration. With that out of the way, I really started to pursue soccer, studying it and playing in a men's league so I could understand it a little more.

Chapter 6:
Military

As I mentioned before, my dad was in charge of all the draft boards in Birmingham after starting out at the one in North Birmingham. He always wanted to serve, but because of his really poor vision, they wouldn't let him. So the only way he could was to be appointed to the draft board. He always felt that we should serve our country in any way we could, and that feeling was passed down to his kids. So my brother went into the reserves, and I went into the guard.

Right after I graduated college in May of 1970, I was sent to Fort Campbell, which borders Hopkinsville, Kentucky, and Clarksville, Tennessee. Many people know it as the home of the 101st Airborne Division as well as the 160th Special Operations Aviation Regiment. I actually loved it, to be honest. Not a lot of people like basic training, but it turned out to be a pretty neat story for me.

CHAPTER 6: MILITARY

When I got there, before we went to the base, we had to go through orientation. And you had to stay in that orientation area for about a week. I talked to some guys there just to try and find out what it was like, and most of them were telling me to get any kind of leadership role I could get. If I did that, it'd get me out of some things that I probably wouldn't want to do. So when they asked me if I ever had any prior ROTC training—which was basically a prerequisite for leadership positions—I told him I had. Of course I hadn't; I lied. But they made me a squad leader, and I thought to myself, "Well, that's good."

And then on the second or third day of basic training, we were in line to go to the mess hall. And when you're in line, you have to double-time until you move to the next phase and then when you come to a stop, you come to attention and then you go to parade rest. The training senior drill instructor saw me doing all that, and he said, "I want to talk to you after lunch." I thought I was probably in trouble for something, but that wasn't the case. By the second day, I had been raised up to platoon leader, and he told me he wanted to promote me to what was called a training senior drill instructor. I told him I was already a platoon leader and didn't really know what I was supposed to do with the new title. But then he sold me on it when he let me know that my new position meant I would get my own room and that I'd be the only man there, so I'd be sleeping by myself in my own room. That was a good deal.

I was going to be responsible for the morning roster and getting everything set up for the day's training, and among other things, I'd be in charge of sick call, taking everybody to get haircuts, and all that kind of stuff. He told me I'd basically be serving his role, only I'd be doing it in the capacity of a trainee. I would even march the troops and learn to count cadence. In order to count cadence, you had to talk from your diaphragm or you could lose your voice. I had never done that before and guess what? I lost my voice for a few days. After that, I quickly learned how to bring my voice from the diaphragm. He liked me for some reason; I really don't understand why, but he did and we got along great. Plus, it was neat to do those things.

One interesting aspect of training is they had boxing back then. My dad had been a prize fighter and wanted to be like his older brother Phil, who fought and was a lightweight champion of the Midwest. When my dad met my mom, she told him, "You can either box or marry me," so he gave it up pretty quickly. His youngest brother, Abe, played professional football for the old Chicago Cardinals, so there was some athleticism in the family. But I inherited my father's love for boxing, and I had done some boxing at home in the local gyms and liked it. Well, there were a couple of guys in my company who were trying to do some really bad things, and I figured the best way to deal with them was to box them. I won a couple of matches, and then I got the hell beat out of me by one guy—I was standing up knocked out; he was beating me so badly. But once the guys saw what I was willing to do, I gained the respect of the rest of the company and we didn't have any more trouble. Before then they would do "blanket parties" where they would take people who weren't pulling their weight, wrap them in a blanket, and beat the hell out of them. I stopped all that. I was already very much of a disciplinarian, so I liked that aspect of military life. And I think the guys respected me too because I never judged anyone by their religion. We're all born the same way, and the way you're raised is what's important.

Each company in the battalion would nominate someone to be put up for what was called the American Spirit Honor Medal. Officially, it's a medallion that "best expresses the American spirit—honor, initiative, loyalty, and high example to comrades in arms." It's a recognition of the best basic trainee in the battalion, which was made up of five companies and over 1,200 soldiers. They put me up for that, and I was flattered just to be nominated. But part of the nominating process meant I had to go before a board and answer a bunch of questions. In basic training they want you to be up on the news, but we weren't really even allowed to read newspapers. So it was hard to keep up with what was going on anywhere. One of the questions they asked me was what happened in a town called Elizabethtown, Kentucky, near where our base was located.

I had no idea what was in the news. So I made something up that was funny, but I have no idea what I said. And they said no, the news was that Elizabethtown had gone from a dry county to a wet county. As soon as I walked out, I said to my first sergeant who was there with me, "Well, I didn't get this." But he had actually stayed in there while they deliberated, and when he came out, he said I had them in the palm of my hand when I made my comment and they were all laughing when I left the room. So he told me that I was going to be awarded the American Spirit Honor Medal. And I got to be on Armed Forces Radio to talk about it, which was also an honor.

Aside from boxing, the whole company had a track meet, and everybody except our company could wear tennis shoes and shorts when they ran. However, we had to compete in fatigue pants and combat boots. We could "unblouse" our pants out of our boots, but that was it. Even so, I ran the mile and actually won the event when I ran it in five minutes. I weighed only 125 pounds then—I'd lost so much weight that I was really light. We also ran the relay; I made a great effort, but we weren't able to win that. Still, that impressed my first sergeant and my senior drill instructor, and I guess that's why they nominated me for the Commanding General's Award. I won it to go along with the American Spirit Honor Medal.

After I graduated from basic training, I was sent to Fort Knox, Kentucky. I trained there as a tanker, which is someone responsible for operating armored equipment. My designation of what branch I was going to be in was 11 Delta 10, and that meant I was an armored scout. The first day at Fort Knox, we sat down with the captain, and he said, "Look to your right, and look to your left. Those of you that go to Vietnam, the life expectancy of a scout is about thirteen seconds once you reach your mission." I decided at that point I just wanted to be a regular soldier. I just didn't want any more leadership stuff.

In basic training I had to get up at 4:00 a.m., go into the office, and set the daily routine, and everybody else got to sleep in until 5:30 a.m. I went to bed in the light and woke up in the dark every day. Overall it was worth it, I think. But later on I went to Officer Candidate School, and that's a whole different story. That was in 1972, and I really wanted to be an officer. I was doing really well, and then I got caught by one of my cadets who saw that I was wearing a T-shirt instead of my fatigue shirt, which was a violation of rules. He reported me to the commandant, and when I met with him, he told me he wanted me to resign—that was one of the ways they weeded out people in those days. I told him that I wasn't quitting. I said if he didn't want me there, he could kick me out. Besides, before I got turned in for breaking a rule, I was first in our unit, so I was obviously pretty good. We had 110 people start, and there were 50 of us left. Then there was some more trouble. There was also a guy who was a senior cadet, and he found out I won all the stuff at Fort Campbell and decided he didn't like that and wanted to beat me at everything. And he literally did beat me outside the mess hall. He would take my hand and put his boot on top, grinding the heel into my hand on the hot blacktop. But I couldn't turn him in because I felt like if I went in there to the commandant to complain, I'd just end up getting kicked out. So I just stayed away from the mess hall, and I had a couple of friends who would bring me food so I didn't have to deal with him.

I did that throughout the summer, and it was tough. But I made it through, and I ended up finishing thirty-sixth in the class. I was busted down close to the bottom because of what had happened, but I didn't quit. I made it through, and that was very important to me. Along the way I encountered some religious issues, some anti-Semitism, from the executive officer. I told him my religion had nothing to do with my trying to be an officer, and we got into a big argument. They tried to get me to quit again. But like always I wouldn't quit, so I just stayed the course.

One other story from that time—the guy who reported me for the rule violation won the Silver Saber (this is the award given to the top cadet in the company based on academic grades, military bearing, physical fitness test, and drill and ceremony competence), which is an award I really wanted to win. The night before graduation, I told a friend of mine, "You stay in the barracks and watch out for anybody coming." And I took this guy outside and beat the hell out of him for reporting me. I felt really good about that. But I did graduate and got my second lieutenant bar. After graduating from OCS, I was selected to be a general's aide or rather aide-de-camp by a former Green Beret, the late General Henry Cobb. This was a real eye-opening experience as basically I was a "butler" for him, doing everything he wanted. Truthfully, he was a new brigadier general and I was a new second lieutenant and neither of us knew what we were supposed to do. We flew all over the place in a helicopter which was fun but very bumpy. The best and funniest thing that happened during my year as an aide-de-camp was that we were in a big meeting with full colonels and General Cobb introduced me to all of them like this, "Gentlemen, I want to introduce you to my aide-de-camp, who is the first second lieutenant in the history of the army that has a general for an aide." Needless to say everyone laughed, and I wanted to crawl under the floor in embarrassment. That was basically it for me in the military. I thought it was a great learning experience for me.

I knew I was spoiled by my parents; I never wanted for anything. The difference is that my parents made me understand I was spoiled. They made sure that my brother and I would work for anything that we attained. Nothing was going to be handed to me because I was Preston Goldfarb. My parents made me understand that nothing comes easy in life, and my father always said, "Plant your feet firmly on the ground, know who you are, know where you came from, and you'll always find your way." And that was so true.

I wouldn't change one thing about the military. I didn't have to pull KP in basic training, and that was the greatest thing for me. But certainly it was a tough time in America. Vietnam War was going on, and even though I didn't have to go there, some of my friends did and some of them died there. The 1960s were difficult years, but honestly, I loved my time in the '60s. I grew up in a wonderful neighborhood, had a lot of friends, which gave me a foundation and idyllic upbringing by my wonderful and insightful parents. It was a real learning time, a great arising of learning what the world was all about.

Chapter 7:

Finding Love

Life after the military saw me teaching at Birmingham University School (BUS)—I coached there as well—and I also started law school. I was at BUS from 1973 to 1975 and started law school in the spring of 1975. Prior to that—in 1974—I went with one of the assistant headmasters, who was head of the English department at BUS, on a tour of Europe. I was asked to go and be a chaperone.

I had just started dating a girl after breaking up with another girl I had dated for two or three years. The girl I broke up with wasn't Jewish, but the girl I started dating was. She was someone I had known my whole life. Well, I was away in Naples, Italy, on that tour, and there was a full moon. There's an old saying in Italy: "See Naples, then die," and that's pretty close to true. So being caught up in the mood, I proposed to my girlfriend from Italy that evening, and she accepted over the phone. I had really only dated a couple of Jewish girls in my life, and my parents always wanted me to marry one. My dad wasn't in great health in 1974 (remember he had a heart attack eight years before that), so I just said to myself, "OK, I'm going to try this." We dated for basically five weeks, and that August we got married. I had just finished my first semester of law school and was starting my second semester. We went on a honeymoon to Hawaii, and I knew right away it wasn't going to work. I mean, it was miserable. We didn't even do things together. I don't really want to get into why it didn't work, but let's just say it wasn't a good thing. And since we didn't get along, I filed for divorce. So in April 1975, seven months after we got married, we got divorced.

While giving the last ever exam to my students at BUS, on May 29, 1975, the school secretary came to get me to answer a phone call. I went to the office, picked up the phone and our next-door neighbor, the late Mrs. Permutt, told me to come home now as it was about my father. When I got home, I saw the ambulance from the funeral home there, so I assumed walking into my house that my dad had passed away, which was exactly the case. My mom was crying, and then my brother (remember he was a doctor) arrived to pronounce my dad dead. It was a tough time for my family, especially for me as my dad was not only my father but he was my best friend and the reason I went into coaching. He was the most dedicated husband, father, and friend, whom I have tried to model my life after.

I wasn't dating anyone at all at that point. After my dad died, my apartment got broken into, and all my clothing and everything was stolen in June. So April, May, and June were tough three months for me. Then in October of 1975, a mutual friend of my current wife, Marie, and mine set us up on a blind date. We went to the old Dugan's bar and grill on the southside of Birmingham. We met some friends there, and we hit it off really well. And when I say we hit it off really well, I mean we ended up dating for nine years. She had moved to Birmingham from Mobile. She was a Catholic girl, one of nine children. So we start dating in October of 1975, and nine years later we got married. I didn't want to rush into anything. What's interesting is that even though my mom wasn't crazy at first about me dating a non-Jewish girl, the more she got to know Marie, the more she fell in love with her and Marie with my mom. Marie basically saved my life as far as helping me get my mental state back and putting me in a good place. At the time she was working with South Central Bell, which later became BellSouth, and she was with them for almost twenty-seven years.

We were at my mom's house in September of 1984, and mom asked, "So when are you going to get married?" And I said, "Well, I think soon." But I hadn't even said anything about it to Marie, even though we had discussed early on. She looked at me and was dumbstruck. So my mother went back in her bedroom and came out with a diamond ring. She gave it to Marie and told us, "I want y'all to have this ring; have it reset to your liking. But if you get divorced, I want it back." That was so typical of my mom, but it was really touching.

Two weeks later we were married. What's ironic, though, is on October 9, 1984, we went to the courthouse downtown and Judge William C. Barber married us. I knew him, and he was a good friend. We got out of there around noon. I called my friend Bill (Corr), but his line was busy. He was in Washington at the time working for Congressman Henry Waxman as his chief of staff. Bill was dating a Jewish girl from New York at the time, and Bill was Baptist. While I was calling him, the line was busy, and I later found out he was calling me. We reached each other that evening, and I told him I wanted to give him some news. He said he had some news to give me too. I said, "Well, I'll tell you ours first. Marie and I got married." And he said, "Well, that's my news too." He and his girlfriend got married, also going to the courthouse, on the same day, which was a Tuesday, making it even more incredible, and neither one of us knew anything about it. We didn't tell each other we were getting married; we just did it. But I married a Catholic girl, and he married a Jewish girl—it's all just really ironic. We went to the old Michael's Restaurant on 20th Street for lunch, and to top it off, we went to my Birmingham-Southern College soccer game that night. It was a perfect beginning.

A year after we got married, we bought our first home. While we were remodeling it, Marie called me and asked if I was sitting down, and I replied, "Why?" She said, "The rabbit died," and I asked, "What?" She then said she was pregnant with our first child. Sean was born on October 9, 1985, and two and a half years later, on March 14, 1988, our daughter, Aly, was born. And it's been a storybook marriage with a storybook courting and a storybook life with my wife by my side. She's supported everything I've ever done, and that's what you call finding true love when someone is there for you no matter what. And it's not about them, it's about us.

My father would've loved my wife, there's no doubt about that. I was just thrilled that before my mother passed away in 2001, Marie had converted to Judaism. My mom knew that, and it made her very happy. And we have two wonderful children who have grown up and been successful (more about them later). You hear people say all the time that their wife is their best friend, but Marie truly is my best friend in the world. We do everything together, and we always included our children in every vacation or trip that we ever went on. We always said, "We don't travel unless our children go with us." Even when Sean was eighteen months old in 1987, we took the Birmingham-Southern team to Germany and Switzerland for our first trip abroad to play games in the summer. Sean went with us, so we packed a huge bag of diapers. And after Aly was born, we took the team to Brazil in 1989 and had the kids with us there. That's the beauty of my wife and how she's supported everything I've done. Even though it took nine years for us to get married, it was just a blissful time and it still is, to be honest.

When we first started dating in 1975, I was coaching my brother's youngest son's soccer team. They had started at the YMCA, and it was miserable. So that's when two other people and I started the Midstate Soccer League. One of the fields we used back then was at the Alabama Boys Industrial School. I helped develop the league and write the constitution for it, and Marie was involved with me all the way through. I remember I was working at University of Alabama hospitals in administration when then Birmingham-Southern College president Neal Berte and then athletic director Robert Moxley contacted me about taking their club to an intercollegiate program. I started there part time in 1983, and I had started my job at UAB in 1979. My first year at Birmingham-Southern, they paid me $1,000 for the whole year. And of course I'll get into more of that later, but my first year there I wasn't sure I was going to stay. But each year they gave me another $1,000. I think the most I made before I went full time in 1989 was $5,000. But even though I was hired as a part-time coach, I was really full time because I was going to practice after work at UAB Hospital and traveling by taking vacation time from the hospitals to coach the team.

Marie stood by me the whole time, but finally she told Dr. Berte's wife, "He can't keep doing both these jobs full time like he's doing; it's going to kill him." And soon thereafter I got called in by Dr. Berte, and he asked me if I wanted to come there full time. I told him I'd love to, but I just needed to stay at UAB through July of 1989 so I could get vested in the teachers' retirement program. So I did that and started full time at Birmingham-Southern in August of 1989. I credit my wife with really pushing that and making it happen.

I've always wanted to be a coach. It was just something that was within me. This is something I've always dreamed of doing even though I didn't dream it was going to be soccer. I thought it would be basketball. I'm thankful for that. The game of soccer has given me way more than I ever gave it; that's for sure. And I give credit to my wife because she stood by me and made me pursue my passion. They would always ask me, "What is your job?" and I would always say, "Well, my vocation is a soccer coach, but teaching the game of soccer is my avocation." I knew I had to leave my wife for trips and she had to put up with me going to Germany usually two times a year to work on my license and to learn from different coaches. Do I regret not spending more time with my children and family? Probably. But they understood, because I included them in everything. Marie supported every single second and every step I took along the way, pushing me even to do more and to get better. I consider myself the luckiest man on earth because I found true love the way it was meant to be in a partnership.

Chapter 8:
CIA

BACK IN THE 1970S, THE CENTRAL INTELLIGENCE AGENCY WAS recruiting pretty heavily with advertisements in the Wall Street Journal. For some reason my late sister-in-law Janet Goldfarb (my brother's wife passed away on August 7, 2019) submitted my name for consideration. I think it was because she knew that I had won some honors during my time in the military and she thought it might be something that would interest me. I didn't know anything about it until after the fact when I got a call one morning from someone in the CIA. The caller asked me if I was still interested, and although I didn't really know anything about it, I played along and said, "Yeah, sure." They set up for me to go to Atlanta and meet with two of their agents—that was in 1979. So I went to Atlanta and I met with these guys and they asked me a series of questions for about an hour—nothing of major consequence—and then they told me they would be in touch.

About six weeks later, I got another phone call and was asked if I was still interested. I told them I was, so they told me to go back to Atlanta and meet with two different people and then see what happens. What they did on this occasion was ask me questions in which they put me in different scenarios and wanted to find out how I would react.

I hadn't even officially applied at that point. But they gave me two applications, and each application was twenty-four pages long. They said, "Here's one to practice on, and here's one to fill out." So I did that and sent it in, and I guess it was January of 1980 when I got a phone call early one morning. They told me that they received my application and once again asked me if I was still interested, and once again I told him I was. So then they said I need to be in Rosslyn, Virginia, at a certain date at a certain time. I was to get instructions once I got there, so I went even though I didn't really know what I was doing or what any of it was about. I had no idea what kind of job they had in mind in terms of where I might fit in.

I got to my hotel on a Sunday and got a call and was told to report to a building on Monday morning where they gave me a physical. That lasted maybe three hours, and then I went back to the hotel. Then I got another message to go to another building on Tuesday at 8:00 a.m. At that point they really started the whole interview process. There were individual interviews and joint interviews, and what I didn't realize was there were people they were interviewing for different positions in the CIA such as geologist, interpreters, and all kinds of different jobs other than field agent. But as it turned out, field agent was what I was being interviewed for. At that time I was fluent in German and French, and I could also read Hebrew, even though I couldn't translate it very well. They gave me a language to interpret, and then they sent me in to a meeting with a little old French lady and a little old French man. And they started talking to me in French, and I was supposed to answer in French. However, I answered in German. My mind was just so screwed up. This was like the third day that I was up there, and I was frazzled. The French couple was really nice. They told me that they knew German and that I had answered the questions correctly, but I didn't answer them in French. I apologized to them, and then that interview was over.

Then I was sent into a room with this very gruff German woman. She started speaking to me in German, and lo and behold, I answered her questions in French. She got really angry at me and stormed out of the room. After that I went in for a polygraph test. The room was tiny; it had a desk and two chairs, and you could reach out your arms and touch both the walls. It was a very lengthy polygraph test, and they kept asking me the same two questions over and over again. One was if I had ever done drugs, and I kept answering no. I was an athlete and just never did anything like that. But they kept saying, "Well, you were around during the 1960s when drugs were prevalent." I told the interviewer I understood that but drugs were never my thing and I just didn't do drugs or drink. Then he started asking me if I had ever done any spying for Israel, and I told him I had never even been to Israel. And he just kept on and on, and it went on for over an hour. Finally it ended, and I was told that I had passed.

Later I went on a tour of CIA headquarters at Langley, Virginia, and it was like walking into a sterile hospital. Everything was just blank. You would walk by offices and look in, and there would be nothing on the desks. And there's a shredding machine on the floor right beside the desks. They took me to lunch at the main lunchroom there. I looked around and all these people had on dark suits and dark ties and none of them wore glasses, and there I was in a sport coat, slacks, striped tie, and glasses. I didn't look anything like them.

One of the questions they asked me during one of my really intense interviews was if I could kill somebody. And I told them that depending upon the situation, I guess I could. What was the situation? So they played a game where the scenario was that I had developed a relationship with a woman in another country. She was an asset, and I was supposed to be gaining information from her, but she didn't know that I was an agent. Of course during all this time, I would have had physical relations with her and everything else, but then once she found out I was a spy, they told me, "You have to deal with that situation." At that point I told them I didn't think my girlfriend at the time (Marie) would like that at all. Anyway, they continued the conversation and kept pressing me on what I should do, and I told them, "Well, I guess you're wanting me to say that I would kill her." And they said, "That's correct; you get rid of her because she knows you're an agent, and you can't have that kind of situation."

They also started asking questions about the Iranian hostage situation, which of course had just happened, and I answered them as best I could based on what I knew. Most of the people taken hostage were CIA agents, and some were marines. Finally I decided to ask them a question, "What if I want to quit?" and they told me that candidates can quit up to a year after they've signed up. Basically when you join, they break you down and then build you back up into what they want you to be. I was accustomed to that from being in the army because that's what they do there too. That's why they want everybody to look alike—shaving your heads and dressing alike and learning the same things. As for the CIA, I'd have to spend six months at headquarters where I'd learn everything I could there. Then they'd put me out on what they called "the farm," and I'd go there for a year. The farm is a friendly foreign country where I'd get a feel for what I'd have to do in the job, and after I had done that, they'd give me an assignment. During my exit interview, they said if I quit I would have to reimburse them for everything they spent on moving me up there. I asked what would happen if I was on a mission and got killed and was told that I'd have a new name and a new birth certificate and would be a whole different person when I'm on assignment. I told him I understood that, but would my family know that I had been killed? They said the CIA would know I had been killed, and the organization would eventually let my family know. I don't really mind dying when it's my time to die, but I told them that it troubled me that my family wouldn't know when it happened.

Another issue is during that first year and a half that you're with the CIA you have no contact with your family unless it's an utter emergency like a death. So when I was offered a spot, I just told him I didn't want to do it. And Marie had told me that if I did do it, she was gone. She knew once I started the process, I would want to go through with it just because I was so competitive. There were eleven thousand applications during my interview cycle, and they narrowed it down to five hundred to bring in for interviews in different cities. Then after that it got divided into a class of 120 divided into two groups of 60.

What's funny is I got some calls from classmates from high school I hadn't seen in twenty years, and they were asking me, "What have you done?" And I had no idea what they were talking about. What had happened is people from the state department had started calling them and asking questions about me. My boss at UAB Hospitals, where I was working at the time, called me into his office because he had gotten a call and wanted to make sure that I wasn't in some kind of trouble with the government. I don't regret going through the process at all because I think I found out a lot of things about myself.

When I was getting ready to leave, I brought them all my receipts from my hotel stay, my meals, and my flight and asked what I needed to do with them. They told me just to throw them away, tell them how much money they owed me, and they would pay me. And they actually went to a big vault and got cash out and reimbursed me right then and there. About a year later, while sitting in the basement of my parents' home, I just decided to call back there and see if there was a chance I could still do it if I wanted to still be considered for a potential job in the future. Not that I really wanted to be considered; I was just curious. They told me they had no recollection of me having ever been there, and then hung up the phone.

Chapter 9:
Hobbies

I HAD BEEN INVOLVED IN PHOTOGRAPHY SINCE THE MID-1970S. I HAD my own enlarger and developed all my black-and-white film, and I even started doing a little color developing. That got too expensive, though, because if you didn't shoot enough film to do it, it just wasn't feasible financially. So I started with black and white and did all my own developing. I set it up in my bathroom in my apartment, and there's no telling what happened to the drains and pipes from pouring all the chemicals down. Later when I started diving, I bought two underwater cameras, a couple of big lenses, and a big strobe and really got heavily involved in underwater photography to the point where I had gotten published in some magazines. While I was working at UAB Hospital, I was also involved in photography there as an assistant administrator. Basically I was moonlighting doing photography for doctors. I had one print titled "Surgeon's Hands." It was a black-and-white print of a thoracic surgeon. I had them turn off the overhead light, and all you saw was the beam from his headlight on the field that he was working on. That picture was put in all kinds of journals, and it was a great photograph.

Sometimes I'd get a call from the hospital in the middle of the night because they would have a surgery that they would want me to photograph. I did some open-heart surgery photographs and other things of that nature. I really loved doing that, because photography was simply a lot of fun for me then, and I still do some now. I used to do a bunch with my dogs, and now I do a lot with my grandson, Otis Wolf Goldfarb, and with my granddaughter, Fiona Jade Goldfarb, my son Sean and his wife Sammy's children. A couple of years ago, I got my first digital camera. I was still shooting film and having to send the film off to get developed. In fact, I still have an icebox full of film. When you keep it refrigerated, it keeps the emulsion from shifting, and it stays in really good condition. I was also collecting cameras when I started getting really involved in photography, and I have old Leica cameras from the 1920s and 1930s. I was just always very intrigued by photography, but I didn't want to do it for a living or anything like that. I loved taking pictures of people. Obviously I would also do landscapes and things like that, but people and animals always intrigued me.

I began diving back in the summer of 1979, starting when my brother's son got interested in it when he was thirteen. He and I took diving lessons in 1978 and took our first trip in 1979; I was there as his proxy. When I got into the underwater diving part of photography, it was really just a natural progression. I'd seen underwater photography before and loved it. I just thought it was a great, great challenge. The camera I used was a Nikonos III. It was Nikon's underwater camera. You could go down as far as 160 feet and shoot, even though I never went down that far. I had a big strobe that I used underwater with it, and I had three big lenses—the last one I got was a fifteen millimeter wide-angle lens so I could get the large creatures like manta rays. It was challenging underwater because the camera didn't have a meter. It was a range-finder camera so you had to guess at your settings, your f-stop and speed, as well as the focus distance.

A guy named Hardy Jones (passed away on December 12, 2018, at the age of seventy-five) had seen my work, and he had an organization out of California called the Living Ocean Society. Marie and I started diving with that group and doing research on different animals, and one trip was to the Bahamas at a place called Abaco in the Gulf Stream where these spotted dolphins would come. They had been studying these dolphins for years. On this trip, Hardy Jones and his wife at the time Julia Whitty wanted to experiment with a mirror to see how the dolphins would react. Upon hearing them argue as to who would hold the mirror and who would film the action, Marie offered to film if he showed her how to use the sixteen millimeter camera. We descended into the water, and Marie couldn't keep up with us because we were swimming against the strong current. Hardy swam back to Marie when she signaled that her oxygen was low and took the camera and motioned for her to go back to the boat. When Marie tried to go back to the boat, the strong current propelled her past the boat, and she became extremely fearful. Then all of a sudden, two dolphins appeared, one on each side, an arm's length away from her, and without any effort on her part, they guided her safely back to the ladder of the boat. Once she was safe, as the dolphins were swimming away, one looked back and winked at her as if to say, "You're OK now." She told Hardy about it when we got back, and he said, "Yeah, the same thing happened to my wife while snorkeling a year or so ago. I noticed that she was getting farther from the boat and jumped into the dinghy to go get her. She had no idea she had drifted so far away. We both assumed that the two dolphins were actually taking her out to sea to be with them."

There was another time we were there when I was trying to get a photograph of this big barracuda, and when barracudas are about to strike, they'll rear their backs up and then come at you. So this barracuda—which was probably four feet long—was rearing up and these dolphins started hitting him with their sonar and shaking him, and the next thing you know, he left. They had sensed that the barracuda was coming at me.

Hardy got involved with studying dolphins and other underwater creatures and started working for CBS, and he was sent to Iki Island in Japan on one assignment. At that time in the 1970s, they were bludgeoning dolphins to death over there. He photographed this, risking his life to do it, and got the video out because he wanted to expose them. He wrote a book called *The Voice of the Dolphins* about his work with them in the wild, and he founded an organization for the protection of these dolphins called BlueVoice.org, which he started with actors Matt Damon and Ted Danson.

We went to the Sea of Cortez in California with Hardy a couple of times to track the blue whale, but unfortunately, we never saw it. We did see hammerhead sharks, and he and I were free diving at one point when we were surrounded by about four hundred hammerheads. It was really special to see them in their environment, and I wasn't scared of them at all. There's another underwater photographer who is really special named Howard Hall; he did some work with Hardy. He gave me his book and signed it, which I really appreciated, and it helped me with understanding how to do photography underwater.

The second time we were in the Sea of Cortez, we were with manta rays. We were on a seamount where the water is filled with plankton, which contributes to the vast number of large pelagic animals feeding. We looked up to see this dark cloud above us, and it was an eighteen-foot-wingspan manta ray. As we learned later, this particular ray had been entwined with a fishing line some years back and was freed by some divers. (A book by Peter Benchley called the *Girl from the Sea of Cortez* explains that very thing). Ever since that time, this particular manta ray, with two remora or sucker fish attached to him, has slowed down so divers could climb on and go for a ride. After Hardy got off, I hopped on for the thrill of a lifetime. This manta ray would wait for you to get on him and go for a ride, and it was unbelievable. Marie was filming it, and all of a sudden, this big eye came up to her—it was the eye of the manta ray. I guess the whirring noise of the camera attracted him to it. But he wasn't going to hurt her. The only way you'll get hurt by a manta ray is if it hits you with one of its wings, and the ones that we were around were just so gentle. They would even do pirouettes.

Once we were on a night dive, and when you go on one of those, that's when everything feeds. I was taking a photograph, and Marie was behind me. She kept trying to get my attention, and about that time I felt something on my leg. It felt silky, but in fact it was two spotted moray eels fighting. My wife's and my philosophy was to bring things up through photography and show it that way, so everyone can enjoy the pristine beauty beneath the sea.

Of course there were some scary situations that occurred underwater. One was at the Sea of Cortez where we were in an area with sea lions. I was photographing them, and all of a sudden I saw this huge sea lion bull—he was probably five hundred pounds and five feet long. He was coming at me with his mouth open. I was scared to death, and the only thing I knew to do was to fire my strobe. When I did, fortunately he veered away. I got out of there and went back on the boat. I told everybody what happened and was informed that I was lucky because that sea lion had just put ninety stitches in a guy the previous week. Another time I was looking into a crevice for something to shoot, and there was an octopus in there. I was trying to get a photograph of his eye, and suddenly his tentacles wrapped around the kit of my camera. We were playing tug-of-war there for a little bit. But as I'd done with the sea lion, I fired my strobe, and he finally let go of me.

I think we stopped diving in 1984 right after we got married, and we haven't been since. But I packed a lot into those short years. The research that we did on these animals and the photos we took, it was just a really special time for me. When you're underwater, all you hear is your own breathing and you see all the beauty of the ocean. It's just amazing to be there and in that environment.

As for my other hobby, when I was a young kid, my dad got me interested in horse racing. He loved the sport, and once you start watching it and realize how beautiful these thoroughbred racehorses truly are and what great athletes they are, you fall in love with it. What I really grew passionate about, though, was studying the bloodlines. I wanted to see where these horses came from and what they could do, and I mainly concentrated on those that competed in the Triple Crown. A guy from Italy, Federico Tesio, wrote a book on thoroughbred horse racing bloodlines, *Breeding the Racehorse*. It was published in 1958, and I bought that book and started studying everything that he had written. It really made a lot of sense to me and prompted me to read as much as I could. I bet I have over fifty books that are biographies of some of the great racehorses throughout history, and in those books, you'll get information about their bloodlines. You can usually go back about five generations to see where it all started, and that's what I would do with the horses I was especially interested in, such as those competing in the Kentucky Derby, Preakness and Belmont Stakes. Mainly I wanted to see how they compared, and what I found was that there were really two tremendous horses early on—Native Dancer and Secretariat. Those were the ones that I fell in love with and to this day still consider the greatest racehorses. Native Dancer had a stride of twenty-nine feet, and they called him the "Gray Ghost." It just amazes me that there was an animal that could basically jump the equivalent of going from the goal line to the ten-yard line. His jockey was Eric Guerin, and he lost by a nose in the 1953 Kentucky Derby, which was really jockey error. But he won the next two races in the Triple Crown, and when he retired, he had won twenty-one of twenty-two races, which is astounding and one of the reasons I fell in love with him.

And of course Secretariat's stride was measured at twenty-five feet, which was also incredible. Based on everything I researched, those are the two longest-striding racehorses of all time.

But really Native Dancer was my favorite of the two, because the more I researched the more I learned that really his greatest accomplishments came through the horses he produced in his bloodlines. He was the damsire of Northern Dancer, which was probably the greatest stallion of the twentieth century, and he produced Mr. Prospector, which was also one of the greatest stallions.

I guess Kelso and Barbaro round out my top-four horses of all time, and of course I've researched their bloodlines as well. And knowing there are only thirteen horses that've ever won the Triple Crown makes me even more interested in finding out where they came from and what pedigree they're part of.

CHAPTER 9: HOBBIES

I just love studying all this. I had very few hobbies in my life, but to this day I still study horse racing. I love it. It's just so incredible how athletic they are.

Winston Churchill said, "The outside of a horse is good for the inside of man." It just makes you feel good when you see such a great-looking specimen. These one-thousand-pound horses have spindly little legs, and you wonder how in the world they can pound on them without doing so much damage every time.

One very special thing relating to this hobby is that during my last year at Birmingham-Southern, Joe Dean Jr., our Athletic Director got together with my assistant coach Greg Vinson, and they thought a great retirement gift for me and my wife would be to go to the Kentucky Derby. The soccer alumni pitched in, and they gave us an all-inclusive trip to the derby in 2016. Joe Dean Jr.'s dad had a box at the Kentucky Derby for years, and he took it over. We got to go into the box and watch the Kentucky Oaks (the filly version of the derby) on Friday, and on the next day we saw the Kentucky Derby. That was such a great experience—that was one of my great bucket list items—and the perfect one for someone who loves researching thoroughbreds as much as I do. They couldn't have given me a better going-away present.

Chapter 10:

BSC Beginnings

IN LATE JULY 1983, ONE OF MY FORMER PLAYERS AT BUS, KELLY Owens, was a student at Birmingham-Southern, finishing up his college work there. The school had had a club soccer team for a couple of years, and it was basically just your typical beer-drinking club-type situation. Kelly was on the team and learned that the school was thinking about moving the program up to an intercollegiate level where they would join the National Association of Intercollegiate Athletics (NAIA) in soccer. At that time Birmingham-Southern had men's basketball, baseball, and men's and women's tennis—those were the only sports they sponsored in 1983. Kelly gave Rob Moxley, the AD at Birmingham-Southern, my number, and I got a call from him asking if I would be interested in coaching the team. I told him I was working full time at UAB Hospitals and had only worked there four years, but I was willing to listen to what they had to say. So we set up a meeting in the first week of August. I went out there and met with him, and he wanted me to start part time, and that fit me perfectly. I had to stay at UAB for another six years so I could get vested into the state teachers' retirement program and wanted and needed to stay there full time. That was very important to me. I was told that arrangement was fine, and I could start at the end of August, meet with any potential players, and take it from there.

Then the AD asked me to talk to Dr. Berte, so I did that and asked what kind of salary they were thinking about. And Dr. Berte told me that it was part time and something new, so they weren't really sure what would come of it. That being the case, they offered me $1,000 to coach the team part time, and I agreed to that. I decided I would talk to Marie, who was my girlfriend at the time, and ask her what she thought. She said if I wanted to do that, it was fine with her, but I needed to talk to the administrator at UAB Hospitals and see how I could work out a schedule. So I explained to him that I've always been interested in coaching and this was an opportunity to get involved in it, but I didn't know if I was going to stay longer than one season. I told my supervisor I could set my practice times, so I asked if it would be acceptable if I came in at 5:30 a.m. and left between 3:30 and 4:00 p.m. Plus, I would have my beeper with me in case I was needed. I got approval for that, and then I called the people at BSC back and gave them the parameters for how I would be able to do it. I'd have to start practice at about 5:30 p.m., and we'd go from there.

Well, we didn't have a schedule, so I had to start putting one together. I called a bunch of teams that were in the NAIA in the area, and I didn't know anything about these programs, to be very honest. But I'd say over half of them refused to play us because when they played the BSC club teams in the past, the matches turned into drunken brawls; they had kegs at the games when they played.

Another big issue was that we didn't even have a legitimate playing field. We had an intramural field that was reminiscent of the lunar surface of the moon. In fact, that's what we called it—"the lunar surface." It had glass and everything else on it, and I wouldn't even really call it a practice field. It was a disaster. But in the middle of August, the college had gotten in touch with some of the players from the previous year and set up a meeting with me at the field. When I got down there, eight people had shown up. I asked, "Where is everybody else?" and was told, "This is it."

So I'm thinking we can't even play because we don't have enough players. I told the guys they needed to go find some more students so we could field a team. I also told them how I was going to run things;

if they wanted to stay, they could, and if they didn't want to be part of it, that was fine too. I basically had four rules that they had to abide by: you don't ever lie, you don't miss training unless you have a valid excuse, you attend class—that means you make good grades and don't cut class—and you give me everything you've got when we're out here. I also told them that there was a no-drinking policy during the season and a no-drug policy forever. If they could abide by all that, then we would be OK. They went into the dorms to try to round up some more players, and I think we wound up with six—half of those had never played soccer a day in their life. With that, we were able to field a team that first year, but it was miserable. We started out 0–7, then we won four of our next seven games, and I think overall we wound up 4–14 that first year. But I hadn't recruited anybody; I'd taken the leftovers from the club team and some players who didn't know what a soccer ball was, basically, so that's how things turned out.

I told Marie, "I'm not sure this is going to last more than the one season before I say goodbye." But I guess the fact that we won some games got my competitive juices flowing, and I thought, "Maybe I'll give it one more season, and next time I can do my own recruiting and get my own players in here."

I told players when they came that they would be building something from the foundation up. When the house has been built, we'll know it's been built when the roof has been put on. Once the roof is on, we'll have a complete structure. So I told these players, "I want you to help me build a foundation by putting the bricks and mortar in first. And you're going to be a part of that. You're going to be a main part of the fact that you helped build this program from its infancy."

So when I first started recruiting, I sold the program on building it from the ground up and letting the players know that they will be in that mortar forever. I recruited primarily out of Grissom High School in Huntsville. They had a really good program and a coach whom I trusted, so the nucleus of our team the next season was out of Grissom with a few more from Huntsville and a couple out of Birmingham. Going into the 1984 season, I knew that we had a good nucleus of players who could help us.

We started winning in 1984. In fact, we had a .500 season that year. So after we had a break-even season I thought, "Well, let's see where we can go with this." I also got married in 1984. We got married at lunchtime and went to a game that night.

In 1985 I went to Germany to get my coaching license and started studying under some of the top coaches in the Bundesliga. I would go back once or twice every year and kept learning and kept learning. By the time the 1985 college season rolled around, I had another outstanding class coming in, and this time there were some players from the Mobile and Fairhope areas, Indian Springs, and some more from Huntsville. With that group we started winning, and we were doing really well. We actually won our conference in 1985 and were making really good progress along the line.

When we began having success, I started selling some of the top players in the country and in Europe based on the fact that they were putting the roof on the house, and that meant getting us to the national tournament. That's when we'll know that our program has been built.

They understood the game and understood how I wanted to do it, and we all improved together. At that time, I thought Germany was playing the game the best. I didn't like English soccer because they played long ball. Coming from basketball, I liked possession.

The ball doesn't have wings on it, so it shouldn't fly—it's not a bird. I felt like the ball was round, and it should roll. That's why I wanted them to learn the game the way Germany played the game. The team that has the ball the most has the best chance of winning. Everybody watches all these great players and everybody wants to be fancy, but I'm not interested in how fancy you are; I'm interested in how smart you play. Soccer is a simple game, and it's meant to be played simply, not fancy.

If you want to be fancy, you can go join a circus. I can train a seal to juggle the ball, so I don't need to see you juggling eighteen thousand times. I need you to learn how to control the ball at different paces. You develop that control by passing the ball against the wall or with each other. Moving off the ball is critical. You pass and move, pass and move, pass and move. That's how you create things. The one play in soccer you cannot defend against is the simple give-and-go. You pass the ball, break, and get it back. If you've got the momentum going forward, the defender is on his heels trying to defend you.

That's how I taught the game. It wasn't about teaching all the intricacies of how you juggle the ball or do back-heel fancy passes. If you did that, you were going to be sitting on the bench because I'm not interested in you playing to the crowd; I'm interested in you playing to your teammate. That's more important to me than anything else—that and how simply you play. Simple soccer wins games, and that's how we were going to win at Birmingham-Southern.

Chapter 11:
More Building

LEGION FIELD IS LOCATED IN McCLENDON PARK, AND IT HAD A recreation field that was situated right there by the fire station on Eighth Avenue North. The Birmingham Stallions of the United States Football League had already come in and developed that area into a really nice grass field. That gave them a place to practice on aside from the artificial turf that was inside the stadium. I knew Walter Garrett, who was head of the Birmingham Park and Recreation Board, and we were pretty good friends. So I went to him and asked, "Hey, can Birmingham-Southern use this field for practices and games?" and he said we could. When there was glass and broken bottles or whatever on it, we'd clean it up, and we would walk our goals down from the campus to the field and leave them there for the season. When we were done, we would get on Arkadelphia Road and walk them back. It was really nice; it was a beautiful grass field that was 120 by 75, so it was a perfect size.

After playing on the lunar surface in 1984, we played at McClendon Park in 1985 and 1986.

In 1986 we had another successful season, so I went to the school president and said, "We've got to have a field on campus—one that we can actually play on."

What we had was horrible. Beside it was an old parking lot that had weeds on it and was overgrown, and it had been a landfill. Even worse, the field was ninety yards long by ninety yards wide. So I talked with Dr. Berte, and he said, "If you can raise the money, we can do it." So I started raising money and talked to a friend of mine, Alan Blalock, who had played football at the University of Georgia and AAA baseball in the Yankees organization. At this point he was a field architect, so he designed the field. We got the best people to make it from Tifton, Georgia, using the Tifton 419 prescription grass. We put it in over limestone rock, which was over a ton of sand, and that meant whenever it rained, the field would be dry within thirty or forty-five minutes because the drainage was so good.

It was 1987 when the field on campus was built, but during the construction process, we were taking the team to Europe to play some matches. We hoped when we got back to Birmingham the field would be ready, but when I saw it, it wasn't what I asked for. The AD had come out and shortened it a little bit from the side and cut off a corner of it. I went ballistic, and he and I got into it big-time. I thought for sure he was going to fire me. I told him it wasn't going to work and they were going to have to redo it, and they did. I mean, I was paying for it, so I didn't care what they were saying. Once they redid it, it was spectacular. It was 120 by 80, which was the perfect size for the kind of soccer we liked to play.

That was really a special year since it was the first on our field. We had another good year in recruiting, especially signing Bill Hughes from Grissom High School in Huntsville, Alabama. Bill would not only go on to help lead our team to new heights and become one of the captains and an academic all-American, as well as a physician, but be one if my all-time favorite players and people. Our first home match was against South Alabama, which was a Division I team, and they beat the hell out of us 7–3. That came after we lost to West Florida on the road to start the season. But we wound up 11-6-1 because we went on a tear, and not only did that make us feel pretty good about the season but it was just so nice to be able to play at home on a nice grass field.

In 1988 I had recruited three German players, and they were three really good players, especially the goalkeeper. We went up to Appalachian State and Davidson and played, and we tied App State 1–1 and Davidson 0–0, but I consider both of those as wins because they came against Division I colleges. They were doing us a real favor by playing an NAIA school. When a school does that, they're not helping themselves; they're just helping you. We also got to go to Notre Dame and play a game after that, but I ended up dismissing all three of my German players after that game. They had done some things that were detrimental to our team. That situation just turned out to be a disaster, and all three left school. But we were starting to build something, and players were realizing what they had to do on and off the field to be part of it. Dr. Berte and I had talked before about me going full time, so in August of 1989, six years after I started the program, I was no longer the part-time coach. It's not every day you get to do something in your life that's not work. It's called work, but it's a passion.

In the summer of 1989, I took the team to Brazil. We had a two-week camp over there and got our butts kicked in four games, but we learned a lot about ourselves. When we came back, we did really well that season and won our conference. In 1990 I took the team to Germany and Switzerland again, and we got to play games and also went to the World Cup in Italy. We had great seats for the match in Milan when Germany beat Yugoslavia, and it was really a great bonding time for us.

That season we were 6–0 in conference during the regular season and playing really well at home in the tournament against AUM (Auburn University at Montgomery), whom we had beaten twice during the regular season. I had two Nigerians on my team that season who were transfers from UAH (the University of Alabama in Huntsville), which was a perennial power at that time. One was an incredible player for us. Well, an article had appeared in the paper the day before, and it highlighted two of my players. One was the Nigerian, and the other was an American kid from Fairhope, George Harrell, who is Birmingham-Southern's all-time leading scorer with sixty-one goals. His picture was large, and the Nigerian's was small, although more of the story was written on the Nigerian than the American. Anyway, the Nigerian player got angry about that for some reason and during the match he had a one-on-one breakaway which would've been a goal and put us ahead, but he took the ball to the corner and just stayed there with it. We wound up losing the game. Afterward I asked him what he was doing, and he told me he was angry about the article. So I dismissed him from the team. That was one of the hiccups we had along the way while building the program.

Backing up a bit, in 1988—before I was full time—I began raising money so we could put some lights up. I had some really good friends at Alabama Power Company who helped spearhead that for me and help me raise the money to build it and put it up. And I had a classmate from high school who was an executive with Sherman Industries, and he helped me get the concrete poles for the lights. I didn't want the creosote poles, because they would eventually rot. Then we raised enough money to get some people from Monroe Electric to actually put in the lights, and they gave us a deal where we paid $60,000 for them. So in 1991 we installed the lights, and that was a really big moment for us. We could play matches so the kids didn't have to miss any classes. The students could come watch us, and it wouldn't interfere with their class time. And a big benefit, of course, was that we could practice around their schedule. We didn't have to compete with class time, and it was just a perfect shift for the college to have that.

By 1991, I had gotten my BDFL (Bund Deutscher Fussball License) coaching license in Germany, and I was really on board with everything. We were starting to grow and really move forward, even though we just had a break-even season in 1991 and a losing season in 1992, mainly because we had some internal issues. In 1993 we finished fourth in our conference during the regular season. All the other teams had international players, and then there was us; we were the only team with all-American players that season. The postseason tournament was played in Montgomery at Huntington College, and we beat Huntington—the number one seed—in overtime on penalty kicks. Then we played AUM in the finals and beat them in overtime, a victory that sent us on to the regional tournament. We lost that game, but we won District 27 for the very first time in school history, and we did it because we had a bunch of unsung heroes out there. We persevered and came together, realizing it was going to take a team effort if we were going to have any success. When we beat AUM, that was such a special win for us because we were finally able to win our tournament.

That year we were not full of great players, but we had great people. They bought into the system, and that was the key to everything. Once we got the lights up, I thought we were really close to putting the roof on the house because we had already built the foundation, and I was starting to get in the kind of kids we wanted to build a program with. These were kids with great character and work ethic, who would work hard in the classroom as well. That's when I finally realized that this was my passion and that I was going to make something out of this program. I wanted to develop a program that would be nationally ranked year in and year out and be respected year in and year out. I decided we were going to be a professional college soccer team, and by that I meant we would look professional and be professional in everything we did. It was going to be first class, or I was going to get out.

That 1993 team made me realize everything was falling into place. I had a saying back then: "There are no superstars on a team; only the team is the superstar." That team embodied that fact because they played as one. There was always a different person who stepped up in every single game in that tournament. That's when I knew coaching at Birmingham-Southern was my passion.

Soccer became my pure passion going back into the early 1970s when I first got involved with it, and it culminated in being a collegiate coach. At Birmingham-Southern I got to start it—I got to birth the baby and build the field, build the lights, and build a program. It was a labor of love, and it was certainly one of the greatest loves of my life.

Chapter 12:
Building a Dynasty

THE YEARS 1994–1999 WERE REALLY JUST SPECTACULAR FOR OUR program. The reason for that is I decided if we really wanted to compete in the NAIA, we were going to have to recruit international players. The NAIA was notorious for having so many teams stacked with international players, and it got to the point where it was just so difficult to compete with them. I felt like I really needed to change the dynamic.

I tried it in 1988 when a former friend asked me for a favor and took in three Germans he recommended. Unfortunately, it didn't work out with them; while they were good players, they did not fit our way of doing things off the field. I dismissed them from the team midway through the season. Alabama football coach Nick Saban calls it "The Process," but what I always called it was "The System." Players have to fit into our system, and it involves more than just playing the game. It involves what happens during the off-season, what you do off the field, when no one is looking to get better, in the classroom, with your family, and with your friends.

So in 1994 I thought we needed to bring in three Germans that I knew—guys whom I had scouted when I had been in Germany. These were young men I was able to spend time with before bringing them in, so I knew them well. One of them I brought to camp to actually work the camp. It was a perfect fit, and he turned out to be an unbelievable player.

At the time the league structure in Germany was Bundesliga One, Bundesliga Two, and Oberliga. Those were the three main leagues. Oberliga was considered amateur, but it really was an elite level of soccer. Holger Schneidt was the first player I brought over, and he was playing in Frankfurt for a club called Rot-Weiss Frankfurt. I had a dear friend over there, Armin Kraaz, who once played for Eintracht Frankfurt's Bundesliga team and for the German under-21 national team. I met Armin in May of 1986, at a game at Waldstadion in Frankfurt, where Germany was playing Brazil in a friendly match, prior to the start of the 1986 World Cup. We took an immediate liking to one another, which continues to this day.

Armin was also instrumental in connecting me with Puma in Herzogenaurach and always took me there to get our teams equipment (I have been with Puma for over thirty years now). He took me to Wiesbaden to see another player, Markus Weidner, who was playing for Wiesbaden in the Oberliga. Markus had said something to Armin about wanting to go to the United States, so we put two and two together and arranged for him to come here. And the other guy I brought over was Jörg Baumgartner; he and Markus were both strikers. Holger was a central midfield player, and he was really the engine of the team. I brought those guys in to fill in the middle and then build the American players around them. My reasoning for that was if I could get anywhere from three to five internationals, I would have enough to make up the spine of the lineup but never have more foreign players on the field than Americans.

I considered 1994 a trial year with bringing back international players after the disaster that happened in 1988, but these were really good people first and they were great players. Holger had some problems with coaches in Germany—he's very opinionated— but I think he saw a chance to come to Birmingham and reinvent himself a little. He wanted to show that he could be coached and play, and he was just an amazing player. He was our free-kick specialist and could do anything with the ball. When the players arrived, they were evaluated based on their German educational experience, which basically went up to the equivalent of thirteenth grade. So when they got to Birmingham-Southern, they were given credit for having two years of college. That meant they would wind up playing for me for two years and graduating in two years. And that's what Holger did. He was first team all-American both years he played and was absolutely phenomenal. Markus was a good striker, but he didn't tell us that he was only going to stay for a year. I didn't know that, and if I had, I wouldn't have brought him over. I got in some trouble when he left. The school wasn't happy with me, but I showed them the sheet he had signed saying he was going to be with me for two years. There was nothing I could do to make him stay. Jörg did the same thing, which really angered the administration and the faculty, so I was treading on some thin ice there until I explained everything. But Holger stayed, and they loved him. He was very bright and did very well academically, so I think that helped me. In 1994 I think we were sixth in the final rankings.

We had gone from not being ranked anywhere, anytime, anyplace to being ranked sixth in the nation. But we lost in the regional tournament, and that prevented us from going to the national tournament. We needed an at-large bid to get in, and we were the last team out. Maybe it was justified; I don't know. There were other teams that made the field that I knew we could've beaten, but it is what it is.

In 1995 I knew we had to add at least two more really good players, and I needed a sweeper, another midfielder, and another striker
to replace the two strikers I had lost. And I also wanted to load up
our schedule with a lot of top-twenty teams. I wanted to play the
best competition out there because not only would it make us better
but our schedule would be so tough it would really help us in terms
of reaching the national tournament. Holger was the anchor and
the spine of the team. And I brought in Michael Morhardt, who
was a really good striker but could also play sweeper, so when we
got a lead against a really good team, he could anchor the defense. I
also added a defensive midfielder, Jens Holtkamp, and he came up
through the youth league at Eintracht Frankfurt. He was playing on
the under-23 team at the time. Then I brought in an unbelievable
striker to go with Michael up top, Oliver Roth. He was a six-foot-
five striker, and pairing him with Michael and Holger helped us
set a record that season. In 1995 we scored 112 goals and gave up
13. Oliver scored 35 goals and had 20 assists, so that was 90 points.
Holger scored 25 goals and had 25 assists. And Michael scored 21
goals up top. We were a juggernaut, to be honest. If we gave up a
goal, I knew we were going to respond by scoring two more. We had
an outstanding defense, led by our all-American goalkeeper Greg
Vinson and our three backs. We played a 3-5-2 system, which was

extremely offensive oriented and very effective, especially with the speed on our wings and toughness of our defenders. It was a perfect marriage between our German players up the middle and our American players around them.

Most coaches want to shore up their defense first and then worry about the offense, but I was just the opposite. I wanted a strong offense because if you have a strong offense, it gives confidence to your defense. Even if they make a mistake and give up a weak goal, they know that the offense will bail them out. I just knew that a strong offense would strengthen our defense, not weaken it. We won twenty-one games that season, and it was just unbelievable. We were playing in the district tournament at our field against Berry College in the opening round; they were an old rival, and the coach of their team was one of my best friends, Kurt Swanbeck. I always love playing my friends. A lot of coaches don't like that, but I do because you know it's going to be a hard game but when the match is over you can give them a hug and everything is fine. We had killed them during the regular season, but in this match they had a plan to double-team Holger so he didn't have any path to get the ball to our strikers up top. It came down to a free kick in the last few minutes, and Holger bent a kick around the wall and into the near post under their keeper, and we won the game.

That propelled us to the district finals, where we played Life College of Atlanta, Georgia, who were predominately international. Their coach was Graham Tutt, a former professional goalkeeper in England for Charlton Athletic and later for the Atlanta Chiefs of the old NASL. He was a good friend as well. We beat them 5–2 and advanced to our first-ever NAIA National Tournament. At the time the NAIA had the best national tournament in the country, bar none. They had twelve teams made up of nine regional champions and three at-large teams. And everything was pool play, and you had four pools of three teams each. The night before it started you had a World Cup–style draw out of a hat, and the top-four teams were seeded. We wound up being put in the group of death.

We were in there with Simon Fraser and Rockhurst, meaning all three schools in the group were top five. That was just bad luck of the draw. We tied Simon Fraser in the first game, and Rockhurst had beaten Simon Fraser by three goals, so we had to win by three goals to force a minigame or win by four goals to advance to the semifinals. Pressure at its best, for sure. We threw everything we had at them offensively and we were winning 3–0, so we were assured of at least a playoff, which is something we didn't want. With a minute to go in the game, Holger was fouled in the box and we were awarded a penalty kick. He scored, so we won 4–0 and advanced. The only negative is that back then they had a stupid rule where if a player had two yellow cards during pool play, he was ineligible for the next game. Well, Holger and our marking backs Phil Harden and Todd Morman had two yellow cards, so they couldn't play.

We were without three starters going up against Lindsey Wilson College of Columbia, Kentucky, who were the defending National Champions and had been our biggest nemesis. It was hard to find an American anywhere on their team. We went up 1–0 on them, and they had a really good striker, Tyrone Marshall. I put a winger, Paul Welch, on him to try and mark him out of the game. Paul hadn't played a lot, but he was really fast. And the Marshall kid was really fast, but Paul did a great job against him and shut him down to the point where Marshall actually spit on him. The referee didn't do anything, and I went ballistic. Then one of our players who saw it got mad and got a red card, so now suddenly we found ourselves a man down against a great team.

Later in the match they got a penalty kick which they shouldn't have because if you looked at the replay there was no foul, but they got it anyway. When their guy took the PK, the momentum of the wet turf caused him to slide into our goalkeeper, Greg Vinson, and his cleats hit Greg and he suffered a collapsed lung. Greg was put in an ambulance and had to be taken to the hospital. Our backup goalkeeper had quit before the season started, so we ended up going with this other kid, Gabe Rulewicz, who played on the tennis team and had only played a little bit of soccer before. But he was friends with a lot of our guys and really loved being part of the team. We had to put him in, and sure enough they got a quick corner kick. One of our midfielders went up to try to clear the ball but headed it into our own net for an own goal. So we lost the game, and Lindsey Wilson went on to win the championship. The funny thing is, we had played Lindsey Wilson in a tournament at our place a couple of weeks earlier and beat them 5–3. The other team in the finals was Midwestern State in Texas, whom we had beat as well 3–2. So we had beaten both teams playing in the finals only a few weeks before. We took solace in finishing in the final four because that was the first time we had ever done that. Had Greg not suffered a collapsed lung, we would've won the game—no question about it. But you know, those things happen.

That 1995 team actually got inducted into the Birmingham-Southern Hall of Fame in 2017, which was the same year I was inducted, and I wanted to make sure that if I got in, that team got in too. It was one of my all-time favorite teams, because everyone bought into the "system" and gave us everything they had, offensively and defensively. It was a joy to coach them. We came back the next season with another one of my favorite teams. We also had a very strong and tall sweeper, Todd Moon, whom I converted from a striker to a sweeper in the back. He was outstanding. Holger was gone because he had graduated, but Michael Morhardt and Jens Holtkamp returned. Oliver went back home and got a contract with a pro team.

I had a Scottish kid who transferred to us from a junior college in Massachusetts in 1996, Sean McBride. He came up through the Celtic FC club and played on the under-16 national team in Scotland. He was a great midfielder. He was like a little engine—a really small guy and his little legs were like pistons going up and down. He was a great leader and a great center midfielder. The reason he didn't go any higher in Scotland is because he tore his hamstring. He was a great person and a very good student as well. We also got one more new winger from Scotland, Stewart McGhee, who could cross with either foot and put the ball on a dime. And we brought in Binni Schram from Iceland, who was a setter for us.

But we were terrible to start out the year. We went to a tournament in Los Angeles early and got drummed, so we realized we had a lot of work to do. We had five internationals on our team, and by midseason we really started to crank up and find our rhythm. We started winning and Lindsey Wilson started winning, and we ended up losing to Lindsey Wilson in the regional tournament. But then we earned a spot in the national tournament with an at-large berth and guess what? We won our pool, made it to the finals, and we had to play Lindsey Wilson again. Our guys were exhausted. We were in a tough group (Houghton College of New York and once again Simon Fraser). Lindsey Wilson was in an easier group, and they got to play a lot of their backup players in pool play. We were down 1–0 at halftime but wound up losing 5–0. We just couldn't click at all because our cylinders were dry. But I was proud of them because we were national runners-up, and we were one player away from being national champions. If we had Holger playing with Sean in the middle, oh my, we would've scored a lot of goals that season.

And we got to host the tournament at Legion Field, which was great. They still had the grass turf that had been installed for the Olympic Games from 1996.

In 1997 we had a pretty good team. McBride was back; Todd Moon was back for his senior season and became an all-American. We had the kid from Iceland, and I brought in a striker from Germany. I had told you about the unbelievable strikers we had before, but this young man, Daniel Nischwitz, was really something. He was playing for Eintracht Frankfurt's under-19 team and could've played Bundesliga; he was that good of a striker. But he was too nice—he never got a yellow card playing in Germany his entire career. He got his first and only yellow card in the last game he played that season with us. Players kept kicking him over and over, so he wore shin guards on the front and back of his legs. I'm not exaggerating either. He was so fast and played very much like Jürgen Klinsmann played. Daniel scored a total of fifty-eight goals over two seasons; that's how good he was.

So I had him up top and Sean feeding him, and we ended up having an OK season. We were nationally ranked, but we weren't a juggernaut. Greg had already graduated, so we had new keepers.

Igor Ranitovic became our best goalkeeper, and he was six-foot-eightout of Yugoslavia. He was a great young man, incredibly smart and made the most of his time with us.

We hosted the tournament again and were in the group of death again. We were in with University Illinois Springfield, which was top three, and Seattle, which was top five. We didn't get out of the group, so that ended the tournament for us.

In 1998 I brought in three more Germans: Thorsten Damm, Marcus Trost, and Waldemar Matuschek. Marcus was a great striker and teamed up with Daniel up top. Thorsten was a center midfielder whom I converted to sweeper. Waldemar was one of best defensive midfield players ever. He just worked and worked. Daniel had another big year and scored a lot of goals and never got another yellow card. We were a pretty good team and very solid in goal with Igor, but our defense wasn't the best. Still we won our tournament, so we made the national tournament again. We won one and tied one in pool play, so we didn't get to go through, which was disappointing.

Going into 1999 Daniel had graduated but still had eligibility and could've stayed and played another season. He was also an all-American and was drafted by the then Dallas Burn of the MLS but decided to return home to Germany after graduation. If he had stayed, I'm confident we would've won the national championship. He was such a key part of the team. But he went back home to Germany, and he later told me that he regretted not staying around for one more season. But that 1999 team was one of my favorites. The players on that team really fit the mold of making the team the superstar. Marcus was all-American, Thorsten was all-American and National Player of the Year, Igor was all-American, but none of them were looking for glory. Still, having three all-Americans in your starting lineup isn't bad. Once again we made it through our group and made it to the semifinals, and who do you think we had to play again but Lindsey Wilson. We went ahead, and they tied. We went up again, and they tied again. In the last four minutes of the game, which was played in Albuquerque, New Mexico, they had a corner kick and a Swedish kid standing on the far 18s (penalty area). They sent the ball up there, and my defender, who had done a great job the whole game, lost the ball in the sun. Their kid took a full volley from the edge of the 18 and sent it into the net. Igor just missed it, and we lost 3–2 in the semifinals. I remember shaking that kid's hand after the match and telling him that was one of the best shots I'd ever seen, and he told me, "I could never do it again." It was a fluke, but it was an incredible shot. If you're going to lose, you want to lose like that. But I was so proud of that team. Overall we didn't have the greatest of players, but we had the greatest of teams. From 1994 through 1999, I'd say we had a pretty good run.

In 1999 the school made the decision to move up to NCAA Division I. Back then you had a four-year compliance period, but the first two seasons you could play a dual schedule in both the NAIA and NCAA.

We didn't play any NCAA teams on our schedule in 1999, but we played a few in 2000 and got our asses kicked. We finished 10–10 that year, which was also the year I got inducted into the NAIA Hall of Fame. The banquet was held before the tournament, which again was in Albuquerque, but it was tough for me because we weren't in the tourney that year. But it was a great run in the NAIA. To this day, I still love playing in that league. To me, it symbolizes what amateur athletics should be about. It's about participation; it's not about rules. The NCAA spends its time trying to catch you doing something wrong. I was happy for the college going Division I, but I was sad to be leaving the NAIA.

Chapter 13:

The NCAA Years

SAMFORD UNIVERSITY WAS DOING REALLY WELL IN BASKETBALL and had gone to the NCAA Tournament, and the media coverage was just outstanding. That's the kind of coverage you can't put a dollar figure on, and it was free. So Dr. Berte and some of the big benefactors at Birmingham-Southern felt that stepping up to Division I would move the college forward outside the realm of Birmingham and Alabama. I think it was the right decision at the right time, even though I didn't necessarily agree with doing it because I love the NAIA and what it stood for back then.

Going into the NCAA in 1999, we had just gotten to our last year of the NAIA, which was also the first year we had gotten to our full complement of scholarships at that level. Prior to that it was always incrementally going up, but we had never reached the full level allowed in the NAIA until 1999. But we made the move, and the transition started in 2000. To go through compliance, we had to reduce our scholarships by 2.1 scholarships, and that's pretty impactful when you're trying to get the best players to come in and join your program. But we were fortunate in the sense that there were a lot of DI schools that didn't have the full complement of 9.9 scholarships, and we did because our school completely funded all our sports to the allowable number of scholarships.

It was a big mess from within the college itself among a lot of the faculty though, because they thought we were spending too much money on scholarships. They said we had 194 scholarships when in actuality we really didn't; we only had forty-four full scholarships that you couldn't break up. That left the rest to be distributed as partial scholarships. In our case we had 9.9 scholarships, and we usually fielded a team of twenty-three or twenty-four players. When you divide that up, we made more money for the college than they were giving us. But the faculty didn't see it that way, so there was a big rift between them and the athletics part of the school for a little while. But we started doing well, and our enrollment actually went up. Students want to go to a school where there's athletic competition and good competition at that.

When we went Division 1, Birmingham had three DI programs in us, Samford, and UAB, so it was a good thing for the college both economically and publicitywise. I felt it was a great fit for the college. To be honest, though, it was a difficult transition for us. When you go from NAIA and lose scholarships and then try to bring in top-flight players who can't play for any kind of championship during the years that you're going through compliance, it's hard. The first time we were eligible to compete for a postseason berth was 2003. Although we were dual members of NAIA and NCAA in 2001, we were ineligible for NCAA championships. It was the same situation in 2002, and we had to play a complete Division I schedule. But once the regular season was over, the entire season was over.

It was difficult to try to recruit kids to come in to that kind of situation. It was a battle for us, and we were struggling. We had two successive losing seasons, and we were just awful. But in both 2001 and 2002, we brought in what I thought were pretty good classes. Still, it was going to take us some time to find our rhythm and figure out how we were going to play in Division I.

When we were in NAIA, we just wanted good people who were good players; we didn't necessarily go after players who were huge athletes—big, strong, fast athletes. And that's what I found the biggest difference was between NAIA and NCAA Division I soccer. The majority of teams have big, strong, fast athletes, and they would play kick and run, which was not how we played. I didn't feel like I could coach that kind of player; it's just not something that you teach. So we stayed within the system that I had developed throughout our time in the NAIA, and we didn't go after the great big players, the great big oak trees in the back. If the player was good and a good person and he happened to be tall, then fine. But if he was short, that was fine too. We just didn't recruit so we could do what Division I was doing. We recruited the way we did because this is what Birmingham-Southern's system was, and we stayed the course with that.

In 2001 and 2002, we played some good teams. We played at Navy in a tournament, and as I've mentioned before, I wanted to play the strong teams. I didn't shy away from them because I wanted to play the best. I wanted to test where we were as a program, and in order to do that you had to play good teams. In 2000 we played Navy at Navy and lost 1–0. That was big for us because they were a good program, and we played them tough. That let me know that we had a chance to be OK in this division down the road. Then in 2001 we had to play a full DI schedule, and we wound up 6-12-1 and just had a terrible season, even though we did beat Pittsburgh. In 2002 we were 5-12-2. We got drummed by Air Force and lost to Denver during a tournament out there, and then we played Navy and were beaten by them 2–1. But we were making progress in 2002. It sounds strange when you look at how poor our records were in 2001 and in 2002, but I felt like in 2002 we were really starting to find our rhythm and how we were going to play to create the flow that we needed. We were continuing losing, and my AD came up to me and said, tongue in cheek, of course, that Dr. Berte wanted to put me on suicide watch because of all the losses. It was a difficult thing for us, but I still felt like we were headed in the right direction.

In 2003, we started turning the corner. I brought in some more really good players that season and a couple of really strong Germans. We wound up second in the conference, and we got beat in the finals of the conference tournament. We were 12-5-4 that year and 4-2-1 in the conference, so that was almost a complete flip from 2002. We played some great teams that year. We beat Navy, so that was a big deal. We beat Saint Francis, tied Army, beat Marshall, and beat UAB. And that leads us to the big story of the year and the most difficult time in my coaching career.

We were playing UAB at our field; they were ranked third in the nation and undefeated at 7–0. It was the ninth game of the year for us, and we had a standing-room-only crowd at our field. There must've been 3,500 fans there. There wasn't an empty spot to be found in the stands or anywhere around the field. You had the hill and all the way around the fence, and people were everywhere watching. UAB had a really, really good team that year, but we had a good game plan for them. I felt like they played some players out of position, because once they got to the 18, it seems like things started to break down for them offensively. So they were pretty predictable on how they played, and we were able to adjust to that fairly well. We had our backup goalkeeper in the game because our starting keeper was hurt. The score was 0–0 at halftime, and we were hanging in there. I had four Germans on the team—four nineteen-year-old Germans. They had just finished high school in Germany, and all four played for Eintracht Frankfurt in Germany on their under-19 team. I had known them for a long time and was able to find the right fit for us by bringing them in. They were just incredible players.

So at halftime, we made a couple of adjustments that I thought we could counterattack UAB with to be successful. I felt that they were susceptible down our right flank and their left side. However, we made a mistake in the middle of the field, and they countered and scored to go up 1–0 pretty early in the second half. But we didn't lose our composure or change our style, and we just kept playing our game, putting the ball on the ground. We had a really nice play that started with a corner kick late in the game. My big striker, Jamie Holmes, was an all-American and a really good player, and he went up and headed the ball in off the corner kick, which was positioned perfectly. So at that point we're tied 1–1, and that gave us new life. The crowd was going bananas, and you could hardly hear yourself think. UAB kept trying to fight back, but we kept winning the ball. Basically, we were just trying to maintain possession and get ourselves to overtime because if we did that, I thought we had a real chance.

In 1995, I found a great free-kick play from the 1994 World Cup that I tinkered with. When Sweden played against Romania, Tomas Brolin was part of the play that was set up maybe five yards outside the 18, and it had to be just off the center of the goal. I named it "play '94," and we scored a bunch of times on it in 1995. What happens is the other team sets their wall, we would put three people over the ball, and then we would put one person on the far side of the wall. You run a player over the ball and another guy would step in like he was going to take it but instead pass the ball on the outside of the wall to our right side. The moment we would do that, the guy on the right side of the wall would break behind the wall and receive the ball with the idea of putting it in the back of the net. It was a really phenomenal play. Well, we ran that against UAB, and it worked exactly as we planned it with Karim Dietz scoring off a pass from Holmes. So we went up 2–1 with about nine minutes to play. And we held on, making that the final score.

Unfortunately, after the game there were some questions brought up to us by their personnel questioning the age of our players and whether or not our German players were actually professionals. It was all the furthest thing from the truth. That was on a Wednesday night, and on Friday we were getting ready to load the bus to go up to Virginia to play Radford and Liberty in our conference when my AD called me and said he had to talk to me real quick. He told me that we had been reported to the NCAA, and I asked him what he was talking about. He said three of the four German players we had on our team were alleged to have played professionally in Germany. I told him that was a bunch of crap but I'd get to the bottom of it. So we got on the bus, and we went up to Virginia while I dealt with this the whole way up. I called my friends in Germany and asked if they knew anything about it. Basically, here's what happened: you can go online, and you'll find something called Transfermarkt. If you pull up a player's name, it will tell you whether they are professional or amateur and if they have an agent or a price tag put on them. None of our players had agents, but three out of the four did have price tags put on them. Five months into this investigation, we learned that that price is called a *"Fördervertrag."* *Vertrag* means "contract" and *Förder* means "education," so it's an educational contract with the club. It didn't mean they were professional; it just meant they had been in that club a long time, and they had put a figure on what they were worth if they were to be signed to a contract by a professional team. All this meant was that if a club bought these players, they would have to pay for how much had already been spent on them for their education. We got a letter from the director of amateur sport of the German Football Association (DFB), and at the top of the letterhead it said "Director of Amateur Sport"; I don't know how much clearer you can make it. The letter said that these guys were not professionals. At that point we sent it to the NCAA, and they wanted to come in and interview our players. The best player I had, Sven Simon, was an unbelievable striker. They interviewed him on the phone, and he told them, "Look, I'm nineteen years old. I'm not a criminal. I haven't done anything wrong. I'm not a professional. I just graduated high school, and I came here to get an education and play; I'm not going to be treated like a criminal."

He left our program. I was furious with him, but I couldn't blame him. They tried to do the same thing to our other German players, but they wanted to stay and prove that the allegation was wrong. I was going back to Germany to recruit and do some things with Puma, and I had to hand deliver a letter from the NCAA to the DFB. I had to take it to the head of football's amateur department, and Germany has laws against releasing any financial data on individuals—they just won't do that. The NCAA wanted to see their actual contract, and Germany wouldn't release it. But what he did was he gathered up these education contracts and sent that information back to the NCAA, telling them that education contracts didn't make my players professional and they were not seen as professionals. As soon as the NCAA got that, we were completely exonerated. It was like going through hell, knowing that any minute you might lose your job and the program could be shut down. And it would be a blight on your reputation for the rest of your life. It was a tough time for us to have to go through something like that. But it made us stronger, and those German players, except for Simon, all came back in 2004 where we were 12–7 and 5–2 in the Big South Conference.

We were basically the same team, and we won our conference. That was pretty amazing considering we had only been really eligible to compete in NCAA postseason play for one season. In 2005 we went back-to-back with conference championships, finishing 12-5-1 and 5-1-1 in the Big South. And we still had one of the Germans who left after the 2003 season but came back to get his double major and played on that 2005 team.

In 2003 we made it to the finals of the conference tournament, in 2004 we made it to the finals of the tournament, and in 2005 we got beat in the semifinals of the tournament. On our way home the next day, we had a horrific bus wreck just outside Atlanta. It was a very traumatic experience for all of us, and luckily no one was killed. We did have some severe injuries among our team. Thanks to our bus driver, Dexter Card, who was able to get the bus stopped somehow after careening against a guard railing. We were very lucky indeed.

Our last year of eligibility in Division I was 2006, but by that time the announcement had been made that we were going to Division III following that season. And while all our players stayed for that final year, it was difficult to recruit.

Chapter 14:
Shift to Division III

IN 2006 WE FOUND OUT WE WERE MOVING TO DIVISION III, AND WE had no idea this was coming about. The only clue we had was when I had contacted a friend of mine who was the coach of Lebanon Valley in Pennsylvania, which was a D3 school. David Pollick had been president there, and he was coming to Birmingham-Southern in 2004 to replace Dr. Berte, who was retiring. My coaching friend didn't have a lot of good things to say.

I wasn't there when they brought him in to interview with all the coaches—I was in Germany recruiting. But before I left, I told our athletic director "Look, I'm just telling you what happened when he was at Lebanon Valley, and based on what I've heard, this is going to be a bad thing for us." I did my due diligence, but the problem is the Birmingham-Southern board of directors did not. Our board was excessively large—seventy-something people—and Dr. Berte believed in having a large board. But he also had an executive council on the board that really controlled everything. The board was really a way to pay back people for donating money and to keep getting money; that's how Dr. Berte set it up, and I thought that was brilliant. But it was a very unyielding type of board. There were six or seven of them on the executive committee led by a pretty artsy guy, and they were the ones who hired Pollick. Pollick and his wife were big into the arts, and they were what the board was looking for. Our AD thought Pollick supported us being in Division I. We were the third smallest D1 team in the country, but we did well academically and were successful. We were doing things the right way, and he thought Pollick was on board with that. I didn't think he was, and I told my AD, "I'm going to give you a little hint. Write it on a piece of paper and stick it in your drawer. In three years, we'll be D3." He didn't believe me, but I really thought that was what would happen.

In 2006, our AD was at a Big South Conference meeting, and he was called to come home immediately. This was in May of that year. All the sports had already signed all their players for the fall of 2006. When the AD got back, he was told that there was going to be a big meeting and that the board was going to vote on whether to move athletics to Division III. So we got busy trying to align ourselves with some people on the board who could help us with the situation, and one of the big benefactors was the late Larry Striplin, who was a mover and shaker who had helped us move to Division I. We came up with the idea of having all our former and current athletes line up so all the people going to the board meeting would have to walk past them and look them in the eye.

Somehow that plan got out, and the person who found out about it went to the president and told him what we had planned. They ended up bringing the board members in through the back side so they wouldn't have to face the athletes. They went into the meeting and voted to go D3 and add football. When that happened there was a call for a revote by Striplin. But the president of the board told him they would be no more votes. They took the ballots outside the room, and it was counted secretly. The assistant to the president counted the votes and came back and said, "D3 wins by three votes." If you believe that, I've got some property I'll sell you. How did they come up with that number? That was just unbelievable to me. So we were voted down to D3, and obviously that made a major impact in the athletic department because a lot of former players who were giving money now refused to give any to the college because of this. It shut down basketball completely for the 2006–07 season, and baseball did as well. Both of these were two of the top programs at Birmingham-Southern for years and years. Basketball was on the verge of going to the Big Dance; they were that close. I tried talking Coach (Duane) Reboul into staying one more season and see if they went to the NCAA Tournament, the media would start to discuss how unfortunate the change would be going to Division III. Maybe that would get the attention of the board and change something. But he said he couldn't afford to have any of his players get hurt and not find another place to go play, and I understood that. Still, it was just incredible what transpired in 2006.

We already signed our players for 2006, but after that season some of them left. I couldn't blame them. As much as I was bitter, I tried to take the high road, and I sent a letter out to all our parents saying that the soccer field's grass is always green, it's the same dimensions, the ball is still round, and we're still going to play. It's still the same game; it's just not in the same division. We played a Division I schedule in 2006, and we were about breakeven. And then 2007 rolled around, and we got into four years of compliance. Considering we had two years of compliance when we were going from NAIA to Division I, that meant we had six years where we couldn't play for anything. So after moving to Division III, we went from 2007 to 2010 where all we could do was play a schedule with no chance at any kind of championship. The 2011 season was our first year of eligibility in D3. At that point I had to get players to come in and play, knowing they had no chance of postseason honors or championships. They just had to play opponents and play for themselves.

The school hired Joey Jones to be the first football coach, and he was a great guy—just a super person. He was at Mountain Brook High School doing an incredible job, but he wanted to get into college coaching. So Birmingham-Southern gave him a chance. But the president of the board said that they were going to spend $1.5 million dollars on football, and that was it. And that didn't do anything. They were building this new stadium, new press box, offices, and all the state-of-the-art stuff, and they only got halfway through it because they ran out of money. They put down cheap artificial turf, and I tried to get them to use FieldTurf because I knew the owner, John Gilman, who has since passed away and it was the number one artificial turf in the world. But the president of the college never used local people to do things; he always brought in outsiders. It was just a real mess going through the change to D3. Trying to recruit kids to play for nothing after we had been a nationally ranked program was, as you can imagine, extremely difficult.

Now you have to tell them that you can come here, get a quality education, and play on a team, but there's no incentive for winning.

There's no incentive other than what you want to make of your experience as a player. If I'd been ten years younger, I probably would've left. But because of my age, I wasn't really tempted to leave. I was already in my late fifties, and nobody would've hired me to go to another program at that age. If I'd been in my forties, I probably would've looked because Division III was not something that I cherished doing. Now D3 up East has some really good programs, but when you get into the South, D3 programs are just filler programs for the colleges to bring in students. We were simply an admission engine, and that's what we were set up to do. We were supposed to bring more students into the college so the college could make more money, and it didn't matter if we won or lost or anything like that. A lot of the players who came in were entitled. They wouldn't come to practice, and you couldn't punish them because that's their choice. They're not getting a scholarship to play, so it was a fine line. But I didn't care about that; you were either going to do like I said, or you weren't going to play on my team. I still wound up getting rid of players during that time because I wasn't going to change the way I did things.

In 2011 we had a pretty good year in D3; 2012 was OK, 2013 was horrible, 2014 was really good, and 2015 was really good.

In 2014 I had two Austrian players, and one was a really good striker. But I just didn't have a good feeling about them. I felt like they were using us for a semester and they were going to leave, and they didn't really like some of our American players. We were in the finals of our conference tournament in Arkansas at Hendrix College and we were playing Berry College, whom we had beaten 4–0 in the regular season. The first twenty minutes of the game, my big striker had three open shots on goal within probably eleven yards, and he shanked all three of them. I could've scored those blindfolded. I felt like it was intentional because he was angry with some of our players. We wound up losing 2–0, and on Monday morning he and the other Austrian player came to my office to tell me they were leaving the program. I just told him not to let the door hit them in the ass on their way out.

We just couldn't get over the hump. We had some good players; there were a few I would've recruited for DI who came to Birmingham-Southern because of the education. Would they have started on my DI teams? Probably not. But they could've been good role players. Players like Garner Shivers, Josh Wild, Jonas Heidrich, Dallas Coyne, Sean Head, Galen Curry, and a few others would have been really good players on our NAIA and DI teams for sure. The majority of our players were really good kids who cared about the program and its tradition, but it became a bad situation for me. I stayed in it until I could retire, which was in June of 2016. My last season was 2015, and my dear friend from Germany, Armin Kraaz, came for my last game because he wanted to be there and show some support. We would talk a lot during the season, and he would point out how great our record was—I think we were 10–0 at one point. But I would always say to him that we were terrible. And I told him if he ever came and watched us play, he would see that. Before that last game, he came to one of our training sessions, and I asked him to just sit and watch it; if he thought I was lying to him, I wanted him to tell me. After practice he looked at me and said, "Oh my God, these kids have no clue." I just told him that we were very lucky and winning games that we probably should've lost.

Besides the 2003 season, my last season was probably my most trying. As I mentioned before, one of my rules was that the players couldn't drink alcohol during the season. No exceptions. During the preseason when we were going through two-a-days, I had never given players the day off, but this season one of the days happened to conflict with the college orientation program. So I knew my guys were exhausted, and I just decided to give them a day off while they were in the middle of this. My last words to them before I walked out of the locker room was, "Do not do anything that will embarrass you, embarrass our program, or break our rules." The next morning I got into my office at about six thirty and one of the security guards, who was a police officer and one of my friends, came into my office and closed the door. When he did that, I said, "Oh God, what happened?" And he told me that the night before there was a big party and a bunch of my players got really drunk. A lot of them were my freshman players. In fact, the paramedics had to be called for one of them. It was just unbelievable. I ended up getting talked out of this by the president at the time, General Charles Krulak, but I wanted to forfeit the season. I was that angry; it was something that I simply couldn't believe had happened. I had three captains, and all three of them had been at the party. I stripped them of their captainships and suspended all the players who were involved. There were maybe twelve or thirteen who didn't go to the party, so we went to play our first game with them. I've never been through something like that. I came that close to forfeiting the entire season in my very last year, and frankly, I didn't care at that point. I'm sure during our DI years there were times when players broke the rules and were drinking, but at least they were intelligent enough not to get caught. But this was just a disaster. It was at the student apartments, and security got called in on it; it was just a complete and total embarrassment. But we weathered that storm and wound up having a good season. It wasn't great, but it was OK.

D3 is a whole different animal. I did a study, and when we started men's soccer in 1983, we had men's soccer, basketball, and baseball, and men's and women's tennis. Those were the only intercollegiate sports that we had. In those five sports, there were probably seventy-five or eighty athletes, and we had 1,300 students. You take away eighty athletes from 1,300 students, and you have 1,220 whom I would call regular college students. When we went to D1, we had to have fourteen sports and we had 190 athletes, and we still had roughly 1,300 students. That gives you 1,110 students who aren't playing intercollegiate sports. Fast forward to D3. We now have twenty-two sports, no scholarships, around 1,100 normal students, and almost five hundred athletes. Now you have six hundred normal students. When Dr. Berte came in 1976, the college was about to fold with a little over seven hundred students. That was the time when there was this high profile murder of one of our students, so there was talk of moving the campus out of Birmingham onto some property off Highway 119. But Dr. Berte said we were a Birmingham school and we're going to rebuild and stay here, and he did it. He built a great endowment and raised the student enrollment to around 1,300 students and saw what athletics could do. If you look at those numbers, you see with NAIA and Division I, the number of regular students were still around 1,100. But then you move into D3, and you're down to six or seven hundred. And that's back down to the way it was before Dr. Berte came along.

If the majority of your students are athletes, there's something wrong with that, in my opinion. When Dr. Berte left, we had something like $150 million in endowments, and when Dr. Pollick left, we had zero endowment. All the money was spent on new dorms, a football stadium, admissions house, on which he put an expensive slate roof. And he wound up putting two speed breakers down twice, because he didn't like the first edition and wanted it to match the roof of the admissions house. He was finally fired in 2010, but the real culprits in all this was the board of directors. In my opinion they were asleep at the wheel and complicit. The difference between a real president, like Dr. Berte, and a destructive president, like Pollick, is really simple. Dr. Berte never built anything unless he already had the money raised. Pollick spent without having the money available. Our soccer program had a booster club that was a way for us to raise money, and we had over $75,000 in it. Then the next thing I knew, we were in a $10,000 deficit.

The school went through furloughs and salary cuts, but fortunately I had an ironclad contract. So I got to stay until decided to leave. When they hired General Krulak, he was a big soccer guy who happened to be on the board at Aston Villa. He came in and did a great job. If not for him, I'm going to tell you, the college doors would've been closed. He got our bond lowered and really brought the morale back to the campus.

I loved coaching, but I just couldn't put up with it anymore. I just didn't like the D3 experience at all. It wasn't fun for me. The final season was bittersweet—bitter in the sense that I birthed a program from its infancy, I built the house from the foundation up, we got a beautiful field, we got a lighted field, we got everything that you needed to make a program successful. That was the bitter part, giving up something that I started. The sweet part of it was that I didn't have to put up with D3 anymore. I didn't have to worry about overcoaching these kids. Like I've said many times, I'm a peanut butter and jelly sandwich on white bread with a glass of milk guy. If you play simply and let the ball do the work for you, you're going to be successful. If you try to do all these fancy things (I called players who did that "Back-Heel Fancy Makers"), I won't put up with that. For me coaching soccer was more than a job; it was part of my heart. It was something I love deeply and one of my greatest loves. It was something I nurtured and built and loved and felt like we were making the progress that we needed to make.

But D3 just wasn't the same. You can teach it the same, and I had some good players who wanted to do it. The majority of them weren't on the same level as the D1 players. It was difficult to get them all on the same page. I never really got along with some of the local clubs because all they teach is winning. I wanted to teach players the mechanisms of how to win. That was the mechanism that was missing when these players came to us. I very seldom recruited from clubs in Birmingham unless I knew the coach. You've got to be able to think on the field. You've got to think before the ball gets to you, think what you're going to do when you have the ball, and then think what you have to do once you release the ball. These kids couldn't do that. You've got to know what you're doing on the field in order to make the team successful.

The game of soccer is such a beautiful game. The thinking of it is like a master chess player, but the beauty of it is like a professional ballet dancer. But you can teach it simply, and if a player does the simple things, you could be successful. Those who are willing to listen could succeed. I always told my players, "Never listen to my tone; listen to my words." I yelled a lot, but I was always yelling about something they needed to do.

Chapter 15:
The Olympics Come to Legion Field

BACK IN 1991 I GOT A PHONE CALL FROM A PERSON AT THE Birmingham Chamber of Commerce. They had gotten a letter from the Atlanta Olympic Committee wanting to know if anyone from Birmingham wanted to attend the meeting in Atlanta about possibly being one of the venues for Olympic soccer. The person at the chamber didn't really think Birmingham would want to do it but was told to contact me at the time, and I said, "Look, it doesn't cost us anything to go over there and listen. It's something I think we should do for the city." I mean, we were talking about a major financial impact on the city with an economic boost if we could pull it off—at least that was my opinion. Kristi Gilmore from the chamber, Scotty Colson, who worked for Birmingham mayor Richard Arrington, and I went over there, and I also took one of my former players, Billy Hughes. He had just graduated and was one of my captains as well as one of my all-time favorite players and people. He rode over there with me, and we sat in the meeting and listened to everything they had to say. We were told that in order to be in the hunt to be one of the host venues, a city had to come up with $3.3 million just to bid. When we came out of the meeting, Kristi and Scotty didn't want to do it, but I said, "Wait a minute. Let's not jump to any conclusions right now. Let's hear this whole thing out." While we were over there, we met a couple of people, including one who had written a bid prospectus for Lockheed Martin Corporation. He was well aware of how to put together a bid. He, Billy, and I sat down and talked about it, and he said he was willing to help us. I told the city representatives that we were interested and the people in Atlanta would start forwarding stuff to us on how to go about handling the bid.

We got the prospectuses from them on what it took, and as you can imagine, it was extremely thick. The city set up what they called a gold-medal committee, and it was aimed at all sports. But they appointed me to the soccer part of it because that was the area we were really going to try for. A guy from Alabama Power was chairing it, and we met downtown. They asked me at that time if I knew anyone with a lot of connections throughout the country and was maybe a name who could help us in our bid. I brought up the name of Dr. Larry Lemak, and they asked me to call him and see if he would be interested in cochairing the soccer part of the committee with me. I arranged that and said that we could make this happen. I let them know that Larry, a sports medicine specialist and orthopedic surgeon, was a money guy and he knew a lot of people throughout the country and in the world.

We decided that we were going to try to raise $3.3 million from the city of Birmingham, the state of Alabama, Jefferson County, Alabama Power, HealthSouth, and some other companies.

The way it was originally set up was the state was going to give $1 million, the city $1 million, and Jefferson County $1 million, and Alabama Power and HealthSouth would split duties coming up with the rest of the money. And remember, this was just for the bid—this had nothing to do with operating costs or what it would cost to put on the event. We, of course, were basing everything on getting volunteers to pretty much run it, but even so you had to have a pretty substantial budget. So we decided once we got the bid and started making money, we would pay back the state and the county before we started looking at the profits for the city from the Games themselves.

At that time, we were setting up for a site visit from the Atlanta Olympic Committee as well as FIFA. I got wind of who was coming from FIFA, and the guy's name was Walter Gagg from Zürich,

Switzerland. Walter was a former soccer player and a really good guy. He was in charge of checking out the fields at the prospective sites, and I remember telling the people on the committee, "Look, if someone from Brazil, Germany, or Switzerland is coming, let me know because I have enough connections in those countries that I can bring someone in who Walter would know when he arrived and that might help us." They would be the first people he would see when he got off the plane, so I did my due diligence to try to make sure that we could put our best foot forward. I knew two people from Switzerland, a guy named Urs Kallen, who knew Walter, and Hans Peter Burri, a good friend of mine whom I met when Birmingham-Southern used to go to Germany and Switzerland and play games. So I told the committee that I've got two guys who will come here and greet Walter with us when he got off the airplane. All we had to do was pay for their flights and their hotels while they were here. I thought that would be something that would really solidify us with FIFA.

They agreed to do this, so I brought both of them over. When we went to the airport, I had them up toward the front, and the first person to get off the plane was Walter. He saw Urs and Hans Peter and smiled immediately, and they all hugged each other. When I saw that I thought, "You know, we've got a shot here." And after Walter introduced himself to everybody, he came up to me and wanted to know how we got two of his friends over here. I just told him that they were friends of mine. And he said, "Well, this is how you win a bid." I knew then we were in good shape, so then we went to Birmingham-Southern and toured our facility and everything was going great. Once we got to Legion Field, we told him that we were taking out the artificial turf and putting in natural grass, and he was excited about that. There was a machine that was going to be placed under the grass that would suction off much of the water if it rained heavily. The field would still be moist, but it wouldn't be really wet. Walter was very impressed by that. Plus, at the time, Legion Field seated more than eighty thousand, so it would be a great venue for Olympic soccer.

Sometimes it's not what you know but it's who you know if you want to make things happen the way you want them to happen. Birmingham-Southern became the Olympic Village, which was perfect because it was right there near Legion field and it just seemed like a great situation.

But we had gone to another meeting in Atlanta, and all of a sudden the dynamics of bidding changed. They told us if we wanted to stay in the running, we had to come up with another $1.2 million. So now we were looking at having to spend $4.5 million just on the bid. I stood up and told them I didn't think that was fair, and

I was backed up by our accountant. But I was told that we were going to do it anyway and was overruled. It was at that point that I decided I couldn't do it anymore. I was constantly butting heads with the leadership, and I just felt like we were caving to everything Atlanta wanted to try to get this, which I didn't think was right. I had my reputation to think about. I still wanted Olympic soccer in Birmingham, of course. I knew it was going to be a great, great thing for our city for generations to come, and I thought it would really propel the city's stature throughout the world. But as it turned out, Birmingham was the only city that gave an additional $1.2 million. The other cities that got spots didn't pay that.

I felt it would be successful, though. I knew a lot depended on which teams we drew, but when our first game was the United States versus Argentina, that was tremendous. Who knows, maybe that extra $1.2 million we spent helped us get that game. But after I left the committee, I was excluded from everything. I wasn't even allowed to go into the Olympic Village on our campus and had to buy my own tickets to see the matches. But setting any bitterness aside, it was great for Birmingham. The level of soccer was raised tenfold by having these games here. I was thrilled beyond words that we were able to land it and make it happen. And if you talk to some people, they'll tell you that the person who was responsible for Olympic soccer in Birmingham was me. I'm not saying that to take any undue credit, but I appreciate that my work was recognized. There was no ulterior motive on my part in bringing the Olympics to Birmingham. I just wanted to raise the level of soccer here and the awareness. That was my goal.

If I had listened to people from the chamber office at the outset and said, "I don't think this is the thing to do," we would not have had Olympic soccer. It would've been dead in the water. But I persisted and it was a big success. Yet I don't think it was as big a success as it could've been if we would've done the things we were supposed to do like pay all the money back and take care of the volunteers like they should've been taken care of.

But that never happened. The only person who really called the bluff on what we had promised was the chairman of the Jefferson County Commission. By that time, I wasn't involved anymore though; I had gotten out. It got prorated and turned into a pretty big stink. I think they ended up getting back 80 percent of it, but that was not what was promised and that really upset me. We had given our word to return the $3.3 million, and I thought we should live up to it. In the end, though, Olympic soccer came to Birmingham. We made something happen that many people thought we shouldn't even attempt to do, so I'm proud of that.

Chapter 16:
Birmingham Grasshoppers

DURING WINTERS IN THE LATE 1980S AND EARLY 1990S, WE USED TO take our team to Atlanta every off-season. The late Mike Balson was a really good friend of mine. He was a former player in England and with the Atlanta Chiefs of the NASL and later became a big-time referee who had an indoor place in Lilburn, Georgia. He used to host tournaments where college and club teams would come in and play. Mike was working with the owner of the United States Interregional Soccer League (USISL)—Francisco Marcos—and trying to help him get the league off the ground. Every time I would go to Atlanta for those indoor tournaments, both of them would keep after me about starting a franchise in Birmingham. Originally I just told them I wasn't sure; because I put so much time in my college team, I didn't know if it would really work for me. And I wasn't even sure I had the desire to do it at the time. But they kept on, and starting in 1991 we began negotiating and getting serious about possibly putting a team together.

You had to put up a $10,000 guarantee from the bank, which was no problem, but still I wasn't convinced it was the right move for me. This went on for a couple of years, with me trying to rationalize in my mind whether I should do it. I had just gone full time at Birmingham-Southern in 1989, so I had to justify whether this would be something that would benefit the players on my college team. And that was the real impetus behind it for me. The college season was short, and this league would give my players a chance to play under my system in the spring. I wanted to keep them under my watchful eye and keep them healthy. If they went off and played somewhere else, I wasn't sure what they would be learning. Plus, what they learned might be contrary to what I taught at Birmingham-Southern. I wanted my players to have a safe place to play and to really advance what we worked on in the fall. So in 1993 I was given a proposal to have a franchise in Birmingham, and of course I had to go to our athletic director and the president of the college at the time and make sure it was OK if we used our field. At that time during the college season, they wouldn't let us put up any signage, and you couldn't have alcohol on campus or anything like that. So we had to negotiate in terms of being able to use signage to raise some money to help fund the club. And even though alcohol couldn't be sold, I'm pretty sure some people brought it in anyway. Overall, 1993 was a bit of a test to see if this was workable.

The USISL set up a league of four or five teams that included us, the New Orleans Riverboat Gamblers,Nashville Metros, Orlando Lions, Memphis Jackals, and Montgomery Capitals. We would play each team at home and away, and it was a very limited schedule. We finished runner-up with a record of 7-6-0.

As for the genesis of the name Grasshoppers, it really was quite simple. After having taken my college teams to Germany in 1987, I wanted to add Switzerland to the trips as well so we could play more games. So in 1988, 1990, 1991, and 1992, we went to Switzerland as well as Germany. It allowed our teams to play friendly games against top competition and thus improve our college teams. It was during the 1990 tour, when we went to the World Cup in Italy, when we stayed in Gstaad Schönried. I became enamored with Swiss football, in particular with Grasshopper Club Zürich. I loved the name and knew they were one of the oldest quality soccer clubs in the world and were very successful. The club originated in 1886, and the origin of the name Grasshopper was due in part to the energy of the players throughout the game. Hence the energetic grasshopper. Their colors were blue and white, but I wanted green and white because grasshoppers were green in color. While the grasshopper was not in their logo, I wanted it in ours.

Simply put, I wanted a great, interesting, and recognizable soccer name for my club. Grasshopper Club Zürich has always been recognized as one of the best soccer clubs in the world, and I wanted to try and emulate their heritage in our club. I don't think I could have selected a better name that I would ever be more proud of. Birmingham Grasshoppers SC was perfect.

In putting together the team, I went through other college coaches to recruit players. I'd ask if they had any players who wanted to stay in state and play during the off-season. We had open tryouts, so a lot of players came in. We were able to evaluate plenty of talent. And of course I knew a bunch of the players because our team had played against them. I'd say that less than 5 percent of our team was made up of players outside of Birmingham-Southern.

The main idea of the Grasshoppers' first season was to see if it was going to work for us. As it turned out, it did really well. We drew fans, not a lot, but we drew more than the college team did. And we felt like we could move forward after 1993. We got beat by New Orleans in overtime in the playoffs, but at that point I felt like if we had a couple of more quality players, we could be a good club.

In 1994 we really went in full bore with it. We decided we would try to make this something really special. During the spring we would have practice after the college team's practice. During the summer when I had my camp, the Grasshoppers would practice after camp was over. We had a really good team in 1994 and did some great things. After the 1993 season, we had to get accreditation from the NCAA to make sure that we were not a pro team. If I remember correctly, we were the only club in the league that was strictly amateur—we didn't have any pro players at all. We had a big fundraiser at one of our games for the children in Rwanda, and USA Today did a story on us for that. Things were going really well, and we made it to the playoffs, which back then was called the Sizzlin' Nine Championship. It was held in Greensboro, North Carolina, where the North Carolina team was based. Of the nine teams that made the field, we were the only amateur club that qualified. All nine regions of the league were represented in the tournament, so it really was a national tournament; we represented the Southeast Region. We didn't do very well in the event; we met our match against all these top professional players, some of them former European players. We just weren't in their league. But it was a great experience for us to make it to the tournament. We were thrilled to be an amateur team playing against so many really good professional teams and players.

In 1994 there was a new team that came in from Hawaii. I met the coach at a league meeting in Florida, and he was struggling to get games. And I told him I would see if I could raise some money to get our team to go to Hawaii. We did that, and we were the first USISL team from the mainland to actually go and play in Hawaii. We played two games there and won both of them and had a great time. Before continuing on the way to Hawaii, we played a team in San Francisco. That club was coached by Lothar Osiander, who coached the US national team from 1986 to 1988, and the whole trip was just a wonderful experience for our kids.

Even though it didn't end so well for us, we learned a lot and decided we would try again in 1995. In that season the league started experimenting with a lot of different rules that were approved through FIFA. For example, they would use kick-ins instead of throw-ins, and instead of penalty kicks, they would use a five-second run from the thirty-five-yard line where you went one-on-one against the goalkeeper, similar to the shoot-out they used in the original NASL. They even experimented with using goals that were higher and wider than regulation goals.

I didn't like it. I'm a purist, and I want to see the game played like it was meant to be played when it was developed. There have been changes over the years, of course, but I wasn't a fan of seeing drastic alterations. One of the experiments was taking away the off-side rule, which was just ridiculous. In basketball we used to call it a "snowbird" where you would take a guy who would stay near the basket and someone would get an easy rebound and throw him the ball under the basket and he'd lay it in. That's basically what you have in soccer with no offside rule. All you have to do is stay behind the defense and look for a long ball. That season we also had some issues with a few of our players and had to get rid of some of them. A few wanted money, and we just couldn't do that because we were amateur. We did allow them to live in an apartment complex next to the campus, and that helped us with the players outside of Birmingham-Southern. We had some players from UAB, the Montgomery area, and even from Kentucky, so we were really trying to ramp the team up a little bit and see if we could take it a little bit further.

The one thing I really noticed about the 1995 season is that when it ended in August and our players would come back to practice for the college team—which was a week after the USISL season ended—they were really exhausted. And at that point I thought I had to reevaluate things to see if this was really what I wanted to do. Do I want to take it further, do I want to keep it as it is, or do I want to say, "Wait a minute, enough is enough!" The 1995 season was good but not great. We made the playoffs, but we got beat early on. So when the college season started, I had to give some of my players who also played for the Grasshoppers time off while my other college players were practicing, and that was a bit of a sticky situation. And then I started thinking that this just really doesn't work. I'd given my Grasshopper players ten days off, so by the time they came back, the preseason was already over. Of course we had that great season in 1995 at Birmingham-Southern, and I started thinking I needed to really put all my energy into the college team.

We started the USISL season in 1996, and we began getting fined for all these stupid things. For example, if our speaker system wasn't working and we couldn't play the national anthem, we got fined $50. We were getting fines for this and that, and I just realized this was not something I could continue to do. Midway through the season, we decided that we needed to end things now. We actually had a virus that went through the team and didn't even have enough players to play. At that time, we were scheduled to go to the Carolinas and play but decided to forfeit those games. The league told us we still had to make the trip and we'd be supplied players from the other team. I refused to do that and got fined $500 for not going on that road trip, and that's when I decided that was it. So we just forfeited the rest of the season, paid all our fines, and that was the end of the Grasshoppers.

CHAPTER 16: BIRMINGHAM GRASSHOPPERS

That was also the year Birmingham-Southern made it to the final four of the NAIA tournament, so it made me realize I made the right decision. But the Grasshoppers were very special to me. It was something I started from scratch. I really wanted to give our kids a little bit higher level of play that would, in turn, help our college team, and it did. Even though they came with the diminished returns of being very tired and dealing with some injuries, it really helped us accomplish some great things. I feel like what the Grasshoppers did was create a different environment for our college team to excel. It accomplished what I wanted it to accomplish, in that it gave our kids a place to play during the off-season and gave them the opportunity to play at a higher level and increase their abilities. I think if you look at what we accomplished in 1993, 1994, 1995, and 1996, I can tell you unequivocally that the Grasshoppers were largely responsible for that success.

Chapter 17:
Preston Goldfarb Field

In 1983, Birmingham-Southern College decided to start a men's soccer program and hired Preston Goldfarb to undertake the challenge of building a new program on the Hilltop.

That fall was Birmingham-Southern's first season of intercollegiate competition, and in this, the thirty-first season for BSC soccer, it is time to honor its Hall of Fame coach.

Preston Goldfarb literally built the Birmingham-Southern program from scratch, raising the money to build the current field, buying balls and soccer goals with his own money, and building a program which today is nationally respected.

At three different levels, Coach Goldfarb has excelled. In the NAIA from 1983 to 2001, the Panthers won ten conference championships, played in the national semifinals twice and the national championship game in 1996. Birmingham-Southern played host to the NAIA National Tournament in 1997 and 1998.

As an NCAA Division I soccer team, Coach Goldfarb led the Panthers to back-to-back Big South Conference championships in 2004 and 2005. In this the third season of NCAA Division III eligibility, the Panthers entered the top twenty-five for the first time after starting the season 6–0.

In thirty seasons, Coach Goldfarb has coached 34 all-Americans, 41 academic all-Americans, and 11 soccer student athletes who have graduated Phi Beta Kappa.

One of the highlights of Preston Goldfarb's storied career happened this past summer, in Jerusalem, Israel, when he coached the United States men's soccer team to the gold medal at the Maccabi Games, the first time in history for the US to win the gold in men's soccer.

Coach Goldfarb has been very blessed to have a loving and supportive family who are here today. His wife of twenty-nine years, Marie, son and former BSC soccer player, Sean, and his wife, Sammy, and his daughter and 2010 BSC athlete of the year, Aly.

It is with great pride that today Birmingham-Southern College officially names the field at the BSC soccer park, Preston Goldfarb Field.

While new signage will be added next week to the scoreboard recognizing its new name, at this time BSC president Charles Krulak will present coach Preston Goldfarb with a commemorative plaque, honoring him for thirty-one years of dedication and service to Birmingham-Southern college and the men's soccer program.

Congratulations Coach Preston Goldfarb!

—From the ceremony held during the official renaming of BSC soccer field as Preston Goldfarb Field on October 5, 2013

That was obviously a pretty special day. They surprised me with it because I wasn't expecting it at all. There were a lot of people there, and most importantly my family was there. Our AD, Joe Dean, and our president, General Krulak, spearheaded the whole thing. It happened in 2013, two years before I was going to retire, and of course they had hoped to have the signage up to coincide with it. It went on the bottom of the scoreboard with my name on it. What topped it off is we beat Rhodes College 3–0 that day, so that made a special occasion even more special.

I was just so thankful that my wife, my daughter, my son and his wife, and my brother were able to come. I had no idea anything was in the works so that made it a really nice surprise. Before it started I saw people at the game that never come to our games, so I figured something was going on—I just wasn't quite sure what it was. After the game when they came over and told me to walk out onto the field with my family, I knew something was different and out of the ordinary. At that point I figured they were going to do something involving me and the field; I just didn't know what it was.

It went really well, and with the ceremony taking place after the game, it was just a really nice event, especially since we got to do it following a victory. As far as getting it all set up, my wife was in on it from the start. I was in Israel that summer with the Maccabiah Games, so all the planning for it was done while I was gone. They had everything ironed out before I even got home in August. Then they decided that October 5, 2013, was when they were going to do it. And aside from my wife and Joe and General Krulak, I know Greg Vinson had something to do with it as well. Since he was my assistant coach for twenty years and a former player who is now the head coach at Birmingham-Southern, you figured he would be part of it. A year earlier the guy who is chairman of the Millwall Football Club in England, John Berylson, donated $1 million to the school, and the soccer park was named after him. So I think at that point since they had what they called the Berylson Soccer Park on campus, they wanted to honor me as well by naming the field for me. Of course when I think about the field, there are a lot of things that stand out.

The first thing that comes to mind is the UAB game back in 2003 when they were ranked third in the nation and undefeated and we won. That was our first year of eligibility in Division I, and the atmosphere at that game was just incredible. There were so many people there, and it turned out to be such a great showcase for our program. Another thing that jumps out at me is 1995 when we had that unstoppable offensive team. We won the regional tournament on that field to advance to the twelve-team NAIA National Tournament. That was the first time we ever qualified for the national tournament, and we did it in outstanding fashion by destroying most of the teams we played against. I remember distinctly having an ice bucket thrown on me and everybody was jumping up and down and hugging each other because it was a first for us to do that. Just so much happiness and emotion, and to be able to do it at our place was so very, very special.

There were some other special memories as well. The first game we ever played on that field in 1987 was big. We beat Christian Brothers, which was a nice way to get things started, and to be able to come out on that beautiful manicured grass was a sign that the program was really heading in the right direction. Running my camps on that field was also so meaningful to me. When you bring in people like Toni Schumacher, Armin Kraaz, Chris Waddle, and Graham Roberts, it really puts your camp on the map. The first time we had one on that field was in 1988. And of course the first time we played a game with the Grasshoppers was on that field in 1993. Our first opponent was the Orlando Lions, and the goalkeeper on that team, Warren Russ, became my assistant coach in the Maccabiah Games in 2013. We lost that game in overtime, but the final score was 1–0; it was really a great contest. Those are the main things that really stood out for me, and I guess I'd have to include my very last game on the field where we beat Sewanee (The University of the South) 1–0 in 2015. There was a big celebration of my retirement after that game, and a lot of my former players flew in from all over the country. My dear friend from Germany, Armin Kraaz, who was so instrumental in helping me get the camp off the ground as well helping me get top players, also flew in to be there for the game.

Obviously having a field named after you is a tremendous honor. So many wonderful things happened from the first time we played on it until that last game, and being a part of it all gives me a great feeling associated with one of the greatest loves of my life.

Chapter 18:
Soccer Camps

THE BEGINNING OF MY TIME AT BIRMINGHAM-SOUTHERN WAS JUST a trial period for me since I wasn't really sure that I wanted to give up the money I was making at UAB to be the coach. And of course, I was part time back in 1983. But after '83 and '84 came around and we had a really good recruiting class, I started thinking about how I could make this work financially and had the idea of starting some soccer camps. In 1986 we decided to do it even though at that time we had just an intramural field and it was really horrible—just rocks, basically—but the school told me I could use that. So in 1986 we did a day camp for two weeks, and it was very cheap for the campers. Each day we'd start at 9:00 a.m. and wrap up by 4:00 p.m., and we provided lunch in the school cafeteria. But in May of 1986, I was in Germany again, studying and talking to coaches and doing some things with my licensing protocol.

That's when I met Armin, who has since become one of my very closest and dearest friends. There was a friendly match between Brazil and Germany just before the start of the 1986 World Cup. They were playing the match in old Waldstadion, and I got to go down on the field. That was where I talked to German national team and Bundesliga star Toni Schumacher—it was the first time I'd met him— and also met Klaus Allofs, who also played for Germany. Armin heard me speaking English and he came over, and we struck up an immediate friendship. So I said, "How would you like to come to Birmingham, Alabama, in the summer? I've put a two-week camp in motion, and I'll pay you to work it." He said he'd love that, so he came and then stayed in my home. He also helped secure and bring to Birmingham a very large and heavy Walker Heading Machine, something most Bundesliga teams used in training. It was a great addition to our camp accessories to help teach our campers the proper technique for heading and who better to demonstrate that proper technique than Armin. He was considered one of the very best headers in the Bundesliga. The rest is history as far as Armin is concerned—what he's meant to me and my career and my family and everything else.

He of course was appalled at the field when he came to that first camp. I told him I couldn't help it but that we were going to raise money and build a nice field adjacent to this in 1987. And that's how it started. We did OK—I think we had eighty kids for two weeks or something like that. But it was strictly a local camp to test the waters. I felt if we did something a little different in 1987, we could make this something special. Having Armin was a huge boost—he was an under-21 national team player for Germany and was considered one of the best defenders in the Bundesliga, always marking the best player from the other team. But when I went back to Germany in 1987, I told him I wanted to do something really unique with a one-week camp. It would only be one week because we wanted to rent Legion Field and hold it there. He said he would come, and I also convinced Schumacher to be part of it. Schumacher wouldn't travel by himself and always had to have someone with him, so I had to pay for his first-class airfare to come in, put him up in a really nice hotel, and do the same for his traveling companion, who in this case was his agent, Rüdiger Schmitz—a very interesting and nice person.

With Armin and Schumacher involved in the camp, it got a lot of attention. I don't know the exact number, but the campers represented in excess of twenty states and three countries. With campers from every state in the US and countries like Peru and Mexico, I had to get the college's approval to house campers in the dorm, and they agreed.

The only problem was we had to walk our goals from Legion Field back to campus, which was a difficult task. Even so, this camp was really taking off, so I started advertising it in *Soccer America*. I had a big budget for advertising and knew if I spent some money there, we could help our camp and also get our college soccer program in the limelight.

So getting Schumacher helped us add more big names—people like Chris Waddle and Graham Roberts from Tottenham Hotspur—and the camp kept growing. We also had Jeff Duback, who was a goalkeeper from Yale who played some for the US national team. But it was expensive to do. Between paying for those guys and housing the players and paying the school for the use of the facility with the cafeteria and indoor pool and everything else, basically all you did was break even.

But I still thought it was worth doing all that advertising. There was a company in Florida that rated all the national soccer camps, and ours was in the top five. Every year we managed to hold that ranking, and it helped us to recruit kids to come to our camp. I sold our president, Dr. Berte, on the idea that if the camps are successful, it's going to be not only a great recruiting tool for our program but it's going to be a great recruiting tool for the college overall.

As we moved to 1988 and had our own field on campus, things really took off. I always wanted my camp to be for both boys and girls. My reason was very simple: it forced the boys to slow down their game and not be so helter-skelter and it forced the girls to try and speed up their game to keep up with the boys. We were advertising like crazy, and in the ad in *Soccer America*, I had a picture of Schumacher with my son, who was eighteen months old at the time; Schumacher was holding him, and they were both winking. When I would go places, people would recognize me and say, "Hey, you're the guy who brought Toni Schumacher to your camp," so I knew then we were onto something special. The next camp I brought Armin and Schumacher back, and this time Schumacher came with one of his sponsors, Gebhard Reusch, whose company was a global sports glove supplier, making ski gloves and goalkeeper gloves. In 1988 we had the camp for two weeks, and we had a field on campus. We usually had about two hundred kids per camp, but in 1988 we had two hundred plus a waiting list of more than 120 kids. At that point I knew that we could do something special with this, and that happened at the same time I was deciding to be the Birmingham-Southern College coach full time and getting excited about that.

Then 1989 rolled around. I was now full time, and I took my team to Brazil. We were in a camp there and played four games, and I met two people who were working with our teams. One was Rui Menezes, who was goalkeeper coach at Botafogo in Rio de Janeiro.

He was a big guy but the most gentle, positive individual I've ever encountered in my lifetime, and I truly wanted him to be a part of our camp. And I met my first world champion player, a guy named Orlando Peçanha de Carvalho. He played with Pelé in 1958 when Brazil won the World Cup. He was a sweeper on that team and one of its captains. This guy was unbelievable, and he helped us at the camp too. So while we're there, I was doing more thinking about how I can incorporate these two guys into our camp and I asked them if they'd want to come to America and work my camp, and they said yes. Once again we had well over two hundred kids, and it was incredible to get instruction from a world champion who had played with Pelé. He started coming to the camp every year.

There was one negative about 1989, though. I was bringing Schumacher back, but when I got to the airport to pick him up, he was a no-show. That became a nightmare because I had to refund money to a lot of people who came from California, Washington, and places like that specifically to work with Schumacher. In all we had probably twenty-five states represented, and with all the refunds, it financially killed me. So it was a difficult time. And to this day I have no idea why he didn't show. Armin ran into him at a bar in Germany several years later and it came up, and Schumacher said he regretted not coming but didn't explain why.

By 1990 we lengthened the camp to three weeks because the number of participants was dictating that. And back then, there wasn't a camp on every corner like you have now. Today some people see it as a way to make a lot of money, to be honest. But I saw it primarily as a way to give kids really good instruction, and it was also a place for our players to work as instructors in the summer.

I would pay them, and they'd use that money when we'd go to Europe. And it gave them the opportunity to teach kids as well, getting them involved in giving back with the camps. We did it as both a day and residential camp, and it really flourished. At that time we became known throughout the country and really throughout the world as a top camp for kids to come learn. And what I named my camp originally was the "Birmingham-Southern College Excellence Through Fundamentals Camp." Later I changed it to "Preston Goldfarb's Excellence Through Fundamentals Camp." Back then people were starting to call their camps "academies" and other pretentious things, but we wanted to teach the game simply. We wanted to stress technical as well as tactical training, and that's what I did.

When I was designing my camp, I decided to do rotating stations during the camp, and I'd design the training differently every day. In 1993 we started getting so many applications for camp I wasn't sure how we could handle it. People were really angry when they were told we were having to put them on waiting lists so early. Laura Malone (1972–2002) was our team manager during her college years and instrumental in helping me figure out how to organize well over two hundred campers each week, so my training grids would flow smoothly. Through her genius of organization, she developed having three grids as water/Gatorade breaks, meaning if there were thirteen grids, only ten would be on the field doing drills and three would be at the water/drink stations. Who was Laura Malone? I'll tell you more about her in the next chapter.

The morning session would be all technical. Let's say we had thirteen groups divided out by ages, so we did 7–9, 9–10, 11–12, 13–14, and 15 and up. We would divide the kids by age first and then we would divide by abilities, and we'd have three water breaks intermittently. We'd block off a fourth of the field for goalkeepers, so that left three-quarters of the field to run our camp technically and tactically. Each station, set up in a grid format, would last roughly twelve minutes, with one minute to move to the next station. So each station would build to the next station, technically, working on different fundamental skills that you would apply in a tactical situation.

After that we'd take a lunch break at 11:30 a.m., have lunch in the cafeteria, then go swimming in the indoor pool, and come back at 2:00 p.m. and start a new session of tactical training.

CHAPTER 18: SOCCER CAMPS

We had both day campers and residential campers, and we tried to set things up so they were divided in half and weren't out there in the heat of the day. After lunch, half of the campers would go watch soccer in the theater at the college. If it was a World Cup year, we'd be watching World Cup games, and if it wasn't, we'd play videos of old World Cup games. The other half would go swimming. Once we were back at our stations, we'd build on what we'd learned. So if we were working on a certain technical drill, we would apply that technical drill into a tactical situation in the afternoon. And we'd do a lot of small-sided things like playing soccer-volleyball, and we would do different kinds of drills. The idea was that what we learned in the morning technically could apply to the afternoon tactically and each day would build to the next day all the way through the camp. I would design these drills differently every day, and there were certain drills we'd do repetitively, such as heading. I liked for them to play soccer-volleyball because I thought it really helped them learn touch.

We would also play games in the evenings, so we would have the little ones playing first, a forty-minute game from 5:30 p.m. to 6:10 p.m. And most of the time we played it with a small size, like 7 on 7, because I truly believe in playing small-sided games—4 on 4, 3 on 3, or 7 on 7—and because you get more touches. It makes you think more than you would if you're playing 11 on 11 where you can hide during a game and never touch the ball. I had some parents complain that they weren't playing 11 on 11, and I told them sorry but that's just not the way we teach the game. I ran my camp that way for thirty-one years. We'd also give gifts to campers who came back, things like warm-up suits, bags, and so on. We had awards for showing loyalty, but I didn't think it was right to give awards for ability because they were all there to learn.

In teaching fundamentals, excellence was the key, and there wasn't a year that we didn't have a camp, even during the Olympic year of 1996. That year I obviously had to work around the fact that Birmingham-Southern was the athletes' village, so I had to wait and run the camp a little later in the summer than I normally did. But the format never changed.

Once they checked in and we brought them onto the field, I would explain what we were going to do and tell them the rules that we would go by during the camp. I made sure to let them know that if they were just here to goof off and spend their parents' money, they're in the wrong place. I told them, "We're going to work you, we're going to make it fun, and you're going to learn the game the way we believe it should be played, which is simple." So I made sure that they understood all this and that this was a working camp.

It was not a conditioning camp. If they wanted to get in condition, they could save a lot of money and do that at home.

Of course I did have some issues with kids during camp. I had to kick some kids out for doing drugs during camp, and we even had a kid attempt suicide one year. It was very scary, and if our counselors had not been doing their jobs, that kid would be dead today. One of my counselors was walking the halls one evening, and I was out on the field practicing with the Grasshoppers. He came running out there and said I had to come help because a kid had taken eighty-something pills as he wanted to kill himself. So I ran up there, and the kid was starting to drop off. We called 9-1-1 so we can get him into the hospital and get his stomach pumped. Sure enough, he survived, and I got a great letter from him and his parents thanking us for being there when he needed us. My counselor saved that kid's life because he was doing his job. All our counselors had rules they had to abide by when they were in the dorm. They couldn't just goof off; they had to be walking the halls, making sure everybody was OK. When I designed my camp, I designed it like I did the soccer program, from the foundation up, where not only are we doing things on the field but we've got to take care of the kids in the dorms and make sure everybody is safe.

Another time we had a couple of kids from out of state our counselors caught with drugs. They were stoned out of their minds, and I told them to call their parents. It was after midnight, but I didn't care. I made them call their parents and tell them to be here by 8:00 a.m. the next day because they were going home. The parents came, and one of the mothers came up and slapped the crap out of one of the kids because he did that. They didn't get a refund either, because that's something we didn't put up with and they knew that. We ran our camp the right way, and we taught it the right way. Vinson now has the camp, and he's carrying on that tradition. It was such a special thing we had. When Schumacher and all those guys were here, we had great media coverage and it put us on the map. But the main thing was bringing those big names here. Initially, it was to get the recognition and renown that we needed throughout the country and the world, and it worked because we had kids from England, Germany, Spain, Canada, Peru, Mexico, and everywhere coming to our camp.

And it wasn't cheap; I can tell you that. My wife did the majority of the administrative work at night while working in a managerial position at BellSouth during the day. She would get so upset with people making changes to their applications because it would cause her to rework so many of the pages. She finally convinced me to add a fee for changes. We left a kind of a map on how to run the camp that Greg and his people call the "bible." Every counselor had a notebook with all the rules. It was so organized that you couldn't screw it up, and that's still the blueprint they follow. They use those still today as a way to teach the game. I just felt like this was something that could give back to the community and demonstrate how we believe the game should be played. Like I say all the time, we're peanut butter and jelly sandwich on white bread with a glass of milk; we're not caviar and champagne. All that means is we do things simply because the game of soccer is a simple game. It's us coaches who sometimes make it complicated. So what we really stressed at our camp was the simplicity of the game itself. What's really interesting is that once it was established, over 75 percent of my college players were recruited from our camp. That's amazing. That's just an incredible number. It worked; it did what I wanted it to do.

It was important for me to use it as a recruiting tool but more importantly, to use it to teach the game the way I felt the game should be taught. Not that my way is the only way or the right way; it's just the way I believe in. It's just amazing to have that kind of legacy for so many years and have a camp that was such high level. To this day, I still have young men and women come up to me and say they came to my camp and how much it meant to them. It was special to have former players send their kids to camp as well. We were not a babysitting service; my brochure outlined exactly what we were going to do. But I wanted it to be fun because soccer is, after all, a game—a very simple game.

Chapter 19:
The Next Generation

THE LOVE OF MY LIFE AND MOST IMPORTANT PERSON IN MY LIFE IS my wife Marie, who I married in October of 1984. Then in October of 1985, our son Sean Ivan Goldfarb was born. When he was born, the dynamics of our life changed for the better. We became a family and were able to exude our love into our children. And Sean was just the perfect child growing up. One of his teachers in grammar school once said, "I wish Sean would just do something bad. He's always so good." He was very quiet as a child but very obedient and very athletic and just loved his family as well. Two and a half years later, our daughter Aly Paige came along. She was born in March of 1988. And with her our family was complete; we wanted two children, and we had a boy and a girl. We were just thrilled beyond words.

We always took our children on vacation. On our first trip to Germany with Sean, we took a huge bag of diapers. I distinctly remember one time we were going from Bremen to Berlin and we had to go through the former East Germany to get there. With all the guards and the people on the fences with their guns, we found a little wooded area where no one could see us and we were able to dump a bunch of diapers in East Germany. That's how we left our mark in that country, which is kind of fun to remember. I also remember having pictures made at the old Checkpoint Charlie that's no longer there, and it was a really special time. When Aly was born, we took her everywhere we went as well. One time we went to Brazil, and that was a really interesting journey on the plane because Marie had just stopped Aly from the bottle and her ears were obviously bothering her. She cried for nine hours, but we got through it; she did well in Brazil. I guess what I'm trying to say is no matter where we went, we always went as a family. As for Aly, nine months after she was born, the pediatrician detected a problem in her heart. We went to UAB to see a pediatric cardiologist who happened to be a person I'd coached in high school basketball when I was at Birmingham University School, and he diagnosed it. But then he moved. So we got another pediatric cardiologist who diagnosed the same thing, and he said he just wanted us to watch it because sometimes these defects will heal on their own. At the time she had a hole that was about the size of a dime between her atriums. So we watched it until she was about seven years old, and then the cardiologist said we needed to do something. In July of 1995, we got the person we thought was the best heart surgeon anywhere because he did surgery for people all over the world. He was at UAB—Dr. Al Pacifico. A friend of mine, Bill Lell, was the cardiology anesthesiologist, and we were friends through soccer. He also recommended Pacifico.

With Aly being seven years old and having to have open heart surgery, it was really very scary. But Pacifico, who had a long waiting list to do those kinds of things, did it. Luckily when he came out of surgery, he said it was a good thing we had it taken care of when we did because the hole was a little bit larger than the size of a quarter. So it had gotten bigger, not smaller, and we were fortunate. They did what they call a thoracotomy, a cut that goes around the back of her bra line, and she came out of it great. But seeing your daughter, or any child, in intensive care on a breathing machine is pretty scary stuff. I stayed with her the night before the surgery, and my wife stayed with Sean at home.

I talk about my kids a lot, but let me talk a little about Laura Malone. She was our manager at Birmingham-Southern, and she was like a part of our family. She had had so many kidney transplants; her father was a Vietnam War veteran and had been exposed to Agent Orange, and she and her younger sister were conceived after he got home. Her brother was conceived before her father went to Vietnam and had no problems, but both Laura and her sister underwent multiple kidney transplants. Laura actually lived with us after she graduated. We made a room downstairs for her, and she stayed with us while she worked for the Southern Company. But then she got transferred to Atlanta. She was an incredible manager for our team. She loved the game of soccer and loved us, and she was a big help with us when Aly had her surgery. She was a big blessing to our family.

In 2002, Laura became very ill and was put in the hospital at Emory. That's where they determined there was nothing more they could do for her concerning her kidneys, and her whole body shut down. She had just turned thirty when she passed away. She had so many challenges but she never, ever complained and always had a smile on her face. She was just an incredible influence on my daughter and my son too, by the way she handled herself and her life in such a positive manner. She was truly a special person. It was a tough time for all of us because my wife's mother had also passed away a day after Laura and our first golden retriever, Nesty, passed away a few weeks later and my mother had passed away a year before that. The best way I can think to describe Laura is from Shakespeare's play *A Midsummer Night's Dream* and the quote was, "And though she be but little, she is fierce." That probably best describes Laura. When we went to the national tournament and got beat in the finals, everybody got rings, and we also gave Laura, my wife, and my daughter a pendant, which was a replica of the ring's top. Laura was buried with that. She loved us more than anything, and we felt the same way about her.

Sean was a very good soccer player growing up. He was extremely fast, and he really excelled. He had to at least learn something just through watching all the games I coached and going everywhere we went. Sean's very, very bright, and he was a student of the game and loved it. We wanted him to really do what he wanted. He played basketball, and he was very good at it but not anywhere close to what he was in soccer. People would often say you can't coach your own children, but I didn't buy into that. I was as hard on Sean as I was on anybody else, maybe a little more so. But I knew from my son that he was going to give me everything he had no matter what. And he understood the game as well as any person I've ever coached in my life and was a coach on the field for me. He went to Cherokee Bend School and then to Mountain Brook in the seventh grade. Later he wanted to go to Indian Springs because of the academics, so he went there and played soccer. I think they were state runners-up a couple of times, and he was a part of that. He helped make that program even better than it had been in the past, and we loved going to the games and following him.

I knew that I wanted him to play for me, but it had to be his decision. He came to Birmingham-Southern as a freshman and was a good player. He wasn't a starter, but he was pretty good. Then he suffered a knee injury and had to sit out a year, but he came back and played well. Sean was extremely instrumental in helping our team win back-to-back NCAA Division I regular season Big South championships. He was such a great student of the game and would always share his thoughts on our playing with me. It was important to me to get his spot-on evaluations to help with our tactical approaches. Without question, Sean was the smartest player I ever coached and my all-time favorite player. But for Sean, I think soccer took a back seat to enjoying college and studying. I wish that he had taken it as seriously as he had as a young player because there's no telling how good he could've become.

He went on to graduate, then took a year off school to work at a law office before going to law school at Cumberland. He did exceptionally well, making one of the law reviews and moot court. He later went to work at my nephew's firm (2012–2014) which is a litigation firm, working on forms of discrimination, equal pay for women, and so on. Sean was doing great, but he absolutely hated litigation because he hated confrontations. Sean's very much like his mom in that regard, which is great.

He has two beautiful children and a beautiful wife, Samantha. They got married in 2011 and have a little boy, Otis Wolf, and a little girl, Fiona Jade. Now we have grandchildren, so that completes the circle. Sean got out of law, and they moved to Tallahassee where Samantha's from. She works with Florida State University in public health, with child care and maternal issues. Sean is now working with that as well, with Florida State University. They can both work from home, which is great, and Sean is doing what he loves to do and especially enjoys going to concerts

As for Aly, she got very involved in athletics after her surgery in 1995. She gravitated toward gymnastics and did really well, but something happened with her elbow—she had a necrosis. So we sent her to St. Louis to a pediatric elbow specialist. My nephew, Dr. Charles Goldfarb, who is a very accomplished hand-and-arm surgeon and goes all over the world lecturing, recommended this doctor. We went up there, and he fixed the necrosis in her elbow. But he said she really couldn't do gymnastics anymore because of the stress. Aly was also really good in track, though, and she excelled in sprinting and running. She also fell in love with pole vaulting, but we had to get permission from her doctor that she could do pole vault because of her elbow. He said yes, as long as the arm that she's putting the most stress on was different from her pole-vaulting arm, and she did that and went on to become a state champion in several events. She had a great track career and got a partial scholarship to go to University of North Carolina at Chapel Hill to run.

We were excited for her; that was where she wanted to go. She had offers from a lot of other places with coaches calling her all the time. But she loved it up there. I went with her on her official visit, and it was really a special place. But when she got there, the coach who recruited her decided to leave and get out of coaching altogether. They brought in a new coach, and things didn't go as she had hope; so she came back home to Birmingham-Southern. The school was starting a track program, and she was instrumental in helping get it off the ground. She holds records there in a bunch of different events, including pole vault, and now she's in the Birmingham-Southern Hall of Fame because of what she did as a track athlete there.

In 2009 she was in the Maccabiah Games as a track athlete and won five medals. She was picked up by a professional track team over there, and she moved to Israel in 2011 to run professionally. She became a citizen there and held dual citizenship with the United

States until she joined the navy and had to give up her Israeli citizenship. In Israel she had to make what's called "Aliyah," which means you become a citizen of Israel. So she went through Hebrew classes and all the stuff she had to do there to become a citizen to be able to compete, and she held the record in the eight hundred and fifteen-hundred-meter runs. Ultimately she stopped pole vaulting because it was dangerous and she needed to concentrate on running. She was picked up by the Israeli national track-and-field team and ran in a bunch of different countries representing Israel, which was a really great for her. But then she wanted to come back home after almost two years in Israel and wanted to be a physician's assistant. She still ran but not competitively anymore, mostly half-marathons and marathons—running distances that I won't even drive.

I think Aly could compete again if she wanted to because she's in tremendous physical condition. I also think she would have been a great track-and-field coach. I discussed it with her, but she said, "Dad, I couldn't be a coach because I couldn't put up with someone that doesn't give everything they had like I did—I couldn't tolerate it." Aly is very demonstrative, very tough, and very competitive, just like her father. She graduated from Birmingham-Southern with really high grades and wanted to go to a physician's assistant school. So she kept after it and worked hard, and she applied to the navy for a scholarship. We didn't really want to her to go into the military, but she is very hardheaded, very driven, and wanted to do that; it was her decision. She got a scholarship from the navy. We paid for her first semester of school, and then they gave her a two-year scholarship in exchange for three years of active duty. When she was stationed in California, she met the love of her life, a marine, Jon Paquette. He got transferred to Camp Lejeune in North Carolina, and then they had an opening there for a physician's assistant. They got married in June of 2020 in Salt Lake City. She and Jon had planned a destination wedding outside Glacier National Park, Montana. But due to the COVID-19 pandemic, it had to be cancelled, and they did an elopement wedding outside Salt Lake City. She now has a job in orthopedic surgery with a hand-and-arm surgeon, which she loves. Selfishly, we truly hope that they'll come back home and have children. But she loves hiking and he does too, so being in Utah is a good thing for them. He got out of the marines, and Aly stayed in the reserves. She's a lieutenant in the navy and loves the military.

It was a special time for my wife and me to raise our children and see how well they've done in their lives now. I've had great loves in my life. Obviously my parents, my brother, his family, coaching soccer at Birmingham-Southern College, the Maccabiah Games in Israel, but the greatest loves of my life is my wife Marie and my children.

Chapter 20:

Very Good Dogs

I'VE ALWAYS HAD DOGS, BUT MY WIFE HAD NEVER HAD A DOG UNTIL we got our first golden (retriever) back in 1996. When I was a child living on the northside of Birmingham, we had a Heinz 57-variety dog named Rusty, and I loved that little dog. He didn't like the garbage people for some reason, though, and he would always bark at them. One day they came by, and he was barking incessantly. I don't know how they got in, but one of them came over the fence and hit Rusty over the head with a board and killed him. I was probably five at the time, and my brother was fourteen. He went inside and got his pellet guide and started shooting at them. I'll never forget that.

That night, my dad called a friend of his and we got a really incredible collie. We named him Rusty too. His background and where he came from was the same as the first Lassie. The guy who bred her was Rudd Weatherwax, who was an actor, animal trainer, and breeder, and Rusty came from that same line. He was an absolutely gorgeous collie. He was the sweetest dog, and he stayed outside during the day. But he liked to go out and get in trouble or whatever, and one night we couldn't find him and got worried because it had been thundering really badly. But the next morning we found him; he had stayed in our neighbor's garage all night. He lived to be eleven and died when I was a sophomore in high school. After I came home from college when I got hurt playing basketball, my brother, who is an international German shepherd judge, was able to get me a shepherd that was the son of the winner of the German championship, which is called *Sieger*. Every year they have a Sieger Show in Germany. The dog my brother got me was the son of the German champion dog. He came from Chicago, and his name was Nestor von Farbenspiel. We called him Nesty, and I got him in 1968. He was the first dog I ever had when I lived by myself. Of course when I went into the army, my parents took care of him.

Well, my brother was going out of town, and he happened to have a female shepherd that we kept while he was away. We didn't know it at the time but she was in heat, and Nesty, who was less than a year old, bred her. They had one puppy, and we kept it and named it Czar; this was in 1969. Czar died at eight in 1977, and Nesty died two years later at age eleven. Both dogs had gotten really bad hip dysplasia and had trouble walking, and we had to put them down.

I didn't get another dog until 1996, when Sean was ten and Aly was eight. We had watched the Westminster Dog Show, and there was a beautiful golden retriever on there. Marie fell in love with that breed. We found a breeder of goldens just outside of Atlanta in Fayetteville; we wanted to get a top-line golden that we could show. She had a puppy for sale, and we went to look. When we got there, we were just thinking about getting a dog but not sure we would. She brought the puppy in, and Marie was bowled over as the puppy jumped into Marie's arms, licking and kissing her and that was it—it was over. Marie became a dog person at that point. We named him Nesty as well, after my old German shepherd, and he was just the most beautiful golden retriever you've ever seen. He was always glued to Marie's side. One evening I was in the shower and he had followed me back there and started barking very loudly. Knowing something was wrong, Marie came running to find the light fixture above our bed on fire. If not for Nesty alerting us, the house could have burned down. I had a friend who had a golden and wanted to breed, but when we tried to do that, we found out he was sterile. But then in 2002, when he was just six, he collapsed. We immediately rushed him to our vet. He couldn't see, he couldn't hear, he obviously had a brain tumor, and we had to put him down.

We were heartbroken but wanted another dog, and I found a really good breeder of English goldens, which are a lighter color, in Columbia, Missouri. We selected the one we wanted, had him shipped to us, and picked him up at the airport. Sean named him Satchmo, but we called him Satch. He would even sleep behind my head on the pillow, so he was my dog. Because I had reached out to many breeders, a top breeder in Green Bay, Wisconsin, sent a photo of a beautiful female. Upon seeing her picture, Marie said we have to have her. We named her Cassie. Satch was not very happy about bringing another dog into the family at first, but they became best buddies. Cassie was always in trouble. She destroyed furniture, she ate a pair of glasses, she would jump on anything where food was in sight, and she did much more. That was her personality. I wanted to send her back, but Marie wouldn't allow that as she couldn't stay mad at her for five minutes. Cassie was definitely my wife's dog—it was unbelievable how much she loved that dog.

In 2005, Cassie and Satch got together and had a litter of seven puppies on October 13. We sold four and kept three, naming them Kol, Kippi, and Max. We named them that because they were born on Kol Nidre, the evening before Yom Kippur. Max, the firstborn was big as a truck, hence his name. Cassie had the best personality of any dog you'd ever want, but she was always into something. Cassie was a wonderful mother and really doted on her babies. She was the sweetest thing. She died on October 31, 2010, and to this day they don't really know what caused it. They think it was a deer-tick bite, but she was an inside dog; so I don't really know. I think it was some type of cancer that got her because goldens are really prone to cancer.

Max was unbelievably athletic. He could jump a four-foot fence with very little effort, it seemed like. He would just be downstairs and spring up on our pool table flat ttfooted. We had a wrought-iron fence on our patio, and it had spears on it. He jumped over it, and when he jumped back, he impaled himself. I was upstairs in the shower when I heard this horrible screaming, so I just put on a towel and ran down there. The other dogs were trying to get after him, which is normal for some dogs. They'll see one in distress and try to get rid of them out of instinct. Kol was really going at him, and so was Satch, although Cassie and Kippi kind of stayed away. I was able to lift him straight up and rushed him to the vet. The spike missed his femoral artery by a millimeter, and if it had hit that, he would've been gone. But they operated on him, sutured him up, and he lived to be thirteen years old. After that, we had to keep them all separated because they would fight.

In 2013, I had hip-replacement surgery and when I came home, Satch never left my side. If I got up to go anywhere in the house, Satch would follow me by my side, barking until I returned to my chair. All our dogs had that kind of instinct and unquestionable love. We had to put Satch down at age fourteen, and Max lived to be thirteen and died of cancer. We got down to Kippi and Kol. It wasn't the same as when Max was alive because Max and Kippi played all the time, but they got along fine. And they loved the pool, looking around and seeing what was going on. Cassie was really the only one who loved swimming in our pool and would do so all day if we let her.

Kippi died on Christmas Eve, 2019, of cancer, and she was fourteen. And Kol was diagnosed with cancer in March of 2020 and lived to be fourteen and a half. Three of our five goldens lived to be fourteen or older, so that was a blessing for us, since goldens usually only live to be ten or twelve on average. When the pups were little and I was at work, Marie would walk all five for thirty minutes every day to tire them out as they had so much energy. One day, on the fifth walk, a woman stopped in her car to ask Marie how long she was going to walk that dog. To which Marie replied, "It's not the same dog; we have five." And the woman said, "Oh, bless your heart." The reason we walked them individually was because they thought they owned the street and would bark and pull if they saw another dog being walked on "their street." After I retired I would walk each one of them a mile separately every day, so there was a time I was putting in five miles a day with them. I enjoyed this immensely.

It is so hard when they get old and you lose them as each one takes a piece of your heart. All our dogs have been cremated except for my German shepherd Nesty, Czar, and Rusty; we buried them in the backyard. I've made plaques for all of them and wrote a little something about them on the plaque. All the goldens from Nesty to Kol are sitting on our table in the den where we watch TV. That was their favorite thing, to be there with us.

Having a dog really turns your house into a home. They're family. But now my wife says no more, so I guess we'll see.

Chapter 21:

Halls of Fame Times Three

T HE THREE HALLS OF FAME I AM FORTUNATE TO BE IN ALL CAME about under pretty different circumstances. I was president of the NAIA Coaches Association from 1998 to 2000, even though I wasn't really looking to do that. But the NAIA was having some issues with leadership and a friend of mine—who had been a friend and competitor of mine in NAIA and in the NCAA Division 1—Bob Gray asked me if I would step up and go in as a vice president. Normally you serve two years in each role, starting out as secretary, then vice president, and then president, but he said I'd only have to do one as vice president and then move into president for two years. The idea was to try and straighten things out within the Coaches Association, especially the rules and regulations concerning internationals and the cheating that was going on. At the time they also wanted to change the tournament from a twelve-team tournament, which was like a real-world copy of the World Cup where you had three teams in a group and four groups. It was really a great setup. There was even a World Cup–style draw the night before the tournament started at the opening banquet for the teams, which usually had a great guest speaker. It was a special time, but they wanted to change to more regions and give more teams an opportunity to participate, making it a sixteen-team tournament held at a neutral site (previously host sites were held on the campus of a member institution, chosen through a bid process with the twelve-team tournament). They didn't know how to go about organizing it, so I was asked to kind of spearhead all that.

After I became the president, we did change some things with the tournament format and made it as good as it could be with the expanded number of teams involved. During that time in 2000, somebody nominated me for the NAIA Hall of Fame in the coaches category. The process is such that you get nominated by someone outside your area, then they do some checking of your credentials, and you get nominated by a committee of sportscasters and' journalists and the like. Once you're nominated, you have to have letters of recommendation sent out, and that's how it happened for me. The ceremony is held at the beginning of the national tournament, and in 2000 it was in in Albuquerque, New Mexico. That was the beginning of our first year of compliance with the NCAA, although we were still competing in the NAIA. Obviously it would've been wonderful for our team to be there the year I was inducted, but we just weren't very good that season. So for me, it was kind of odd to be there. We'd been to the tournament every year since 1995 but didn't get in in 2000 and frankly didn't deserve to be there. But I went in with a good friend of mine who coached at what's now known as Illinois-Springfield, Aydin Gonulsen, so that made it special. The best thing about that induction was that my family was there to support me, along with my assistant coach and former player, Greg Vinson, as well as my former athletic director (1993–1999), Mike Robinson.

As for Birmingham-Southern, there's a Hall of Fame committee that I was actually on, but obviously I had to recuse myself when I found out I had been nominated for the Birmingham-Southern Athletics Hall of Fame. In order to get in as a coach, you have to be out of coaching for at least a year. This was in 2017, and it was basically one year after I retired. But my daughter went in in 2016, and I didn't want to go in with her and take away from what she had accomplished. I wanted her to stand on her own, so my induction got delayed a year. And I was very honored, of course, because being able to build the soccer program from the ground up and having so many wonderful years as coach is something that will always be so rewarding. Any time you're honored in this way it means so much, and to be honored by the school that I spent thirty-three years at was a great feeling. This honor was made even more special, in that my family was there, as well as my brother, Morton, his late wife, Janet, and his son, Jon, and his wife, Melina. But the real highlights—at least to me—were when my son, Sean, gave a very moving speech inducting me into the Birmingham-Southern College Hall of Fame. And my daughter Aly, who couldn't be there because she was on active duty in the navy stationed at Twentynine Palms, California, sent a very heartfelt taped message. Also being inducted along with me was our 1995 team, (with most players attending and coming from as far away as Germany), which was the first to go to the NAIA National Tournament and finish in the final four. It truly was a wonderful evening sharing this honor with my family and my 1995 team.

But then that summer I had gone to Israel to coach the Maccabiah Games, and when I got home in August, there was a letter waiting for me from the Jewish Sports Heritage Hall of Fame in New York. It said that not only had I been nominated for that Hall of Fame but was to be inducted in April of 2018 along with Olympic swimming champion Dara Torres (as well as Cliff Bayer, fencing; Boyd Melson, boxing; Merrill Moses, water polo; Vic Niederhoffer, squash; Tracie Max Sachs, speed skiing; and Roby Young, soccer). I was just flabbergasted that I was going in with legends like Sandy Koufax and Red Auerbach. I was flattered and humbled and honored. My family and I flew to New York, and there was a ceremony on Sunday morning. The Jewish Sports Heritage Association was actually a new version of what was once called the Jewish Sports Hall of Fame. They used to have inductions every year but then stopped, and starting in 2018 they began doing it again.

So the three halls of fame I'm in are Birmingham-Southern, which I went in in 2017 and was inducted into the same date that they named the field after me, the NAIA Hall of Fame induction in 2000, and the Jewish Heritage Hall of Fame in 2018.

They all mean a lot of course. Honestly I basically knew I was getting in the Birmingham-Southern Hall of Fame. I'm not saying that to boast, but some of the things we accomplished led to that. And making the NAIA meant a lot because I was recognized as both a coach and also for the things I accomplished as president, changing some things around to make it better for the student athletes to compete and have more chances to play in the national tournament.

But the most meaningful would have to be the Jewish Sports Heritage Hall of Fame. That just came out of the clear blue—I had absolutely no idea about that and couldn't believe I would even be considered. One thing I remember is at the ceremony, the person in charge of it got up and said some years before that I had been sent a letter asking about possibly helping someone from New York come to one of my soccer camps but that person couldn't afford it, so I'd need to issue a certificate that would allow him to come for free. He was the one who sent that letter and helped get that individual to our camp, so that was kind of fun. Just getting into a national Hall of Fame was just so humbling to me. I guess the fact that I had a reasonable career at Birmingham-Southern helped, but more importantly, I'd had two really successful runs in the Maccabiah Games; no other American coach had ever led their teams to two gold medals in the eighty-year history of the Games. Still, how in the world does someone like me get in? And it didn't just honor me, but it honored my family. I still have no idea how they researched me and decided to induct me, but it'll always be something I'm so proud of. The person who really revived the Jewish Heritage Sports Hall of Fame is named Alan Freedman, a really nice person but more importantly, a visionary for Jewish athletes, coaches, and people who have had impacts on their respective sports. He started this thing after the original Jewish Hall of Fame had kind of faded away and turned it into something special. Each year all the inductees get invited back to the next event, so you're always a part of it. With respect to these very humbling honors, all I can say is I've been extremely lucky.

Chapter 22:
Maccabiah Beginnings

My association with the Maccabiah Games started back 2001, and things didn't get off to a very good start. I had gotten a call from someone affiliated with Maccabi USA about coaching a youth team in the Games, and I agreed. We even selected a team. But then all of a sudden war broke out in Israel and this town where we were supposed to stay in, Netanya, near Tel Aviv, had experienced bombing and all sorts of violence. Years before when I took a coaching course in Germany, I met Zeev Zeltzer, who was a former Israeli soccer player and an Israeli national coach of pretty high prominence. With everything going on with the war, I called him up and asked him if it was safe to take a team there. He said there had been a cafe bombed near where we would be staying and people were killed and if he were me, he wouldn't come because it's just too dangerous. And I was getting calls from worried parents wondering about the danger to their kids and they didn't really want to go, and I didn't blame them. So I called a man who was an executive on the board of Maccabi USA and told him I was going to have to back out, and we got into it over the phone. He was extremely angry that I had decided not to bring a team there, and I just told him I wasn't going to endanger the lives of the kids or my son Sean, who was playing on the team, or myself. I also told him about talking to Zeev and what he said about the situation, but the guy didn't care.

All the other soccer coaches had abandoned ship too, but I guess since I was the last coach to pull out, it set him off. But they found some fill-in coaches to take over the teams and the games went on, and that was that. It wasn't a huge success, though, in terms of people who participated and the number of countries involved. Regardless, I did what I thought was right and was satisfied with my decision. In 2005 I got another call from a guy who was the chairman of the youth team, and he asked me if I would be interested in coaching. I was, but I told him that before we went any further, he needed to talk to Maccabi USA and the new program director, Ami Monson, to see if they'll allow me to do it and my guess is they won't because of me pulling out a few years earlier. A little later he called me and said I was right; I wouldn't be allowed to coach because of what happened in 2001. It was interesting because a lot of the other coaches who had backed out were welcomed back with open arms, but I wasn't. I was told the reason was that I had been blackballed by that one person, and I just assumed that was the end of it. Of course I heard they ended up selecting another coach, and it was a disaster. He didn't spend time with the kids, and it turned out to be a horrible experience for them. I'm not going to use his name, but he's still coaching today in the United States. And later I was told he'd never be allowed to coach in the Maccabiah Games again because of how bad it was in 2005.

Jump to 2008 and I'm at the National Soccer Coaches Association of America (it's now called the United Soccer Coaches) convention in Philadelphia. And they have booths set up and exhibit halls, and I saw a friend who took me over to a Maccabi booth to meet Monson, whom I mentioned from when he started in 2005. We started talking, and he told me a new person was in charge of Maccabi USA programs and responsible for selecting coaches. The new person in charge of all soccer teams was Mark Knue, and he and I became very close and dear friends from that point to this day. Just like in 2001 and 2005, I was asked about coaching. I said, "Look, I've already been thrown under the bus, and I don't need to be thrown under the bus a second time. I'm just not interested." But then I was told that the guy who blackballed me was no longer involved at all and that they really wanted me to be a part of it. So I agreed again, but only if my son could come with me as an assistant; they agreed to that. So in 2009 we coached the juniors team, which was an under-16 team, and I thought it was a good experience and a good thing to do to get back into it. My son was there with me; my daughter, who was selected to run and pole vault for the track-and-field team, was also there. Coaching this team gave me an idea of what to expect in these types of games.

The teams got to go there four days before the delegation did, so during that time we got to train and get to know each other and see so many wonderful things. The Maccabiah Games allows kids to come to Israel to explore their heritage and tour the country, which is just spectacular. We'd train early in the morning and have the rest of the day and evening to go to all the major points. Obviously there was the Western Wall, which is also known as the Wailing Wall, and we did some other neat things, including going to the Sea of Galilee.

Israel also has what's known as the Birthright Program, which means anyone under the age of twenty-five can go to Israel free for ten days, so a lot of the players we had took advantage of that. It's something special and really fits into the Maccabi mission of learning about heritage and history. To be able to explore that through sport is just incredible. Not only do you learn about Israel but also you learn about other countries and cultures through your interactions.

Behind the Olympics and the Pan-American Games, this is the third largest sporting event of its kind in the world, so it's a very big deal. You have over eighty countries represented now, and it's sanctioned by the United States Olympic Committee. Just like the Olympics, you have an opening ceremony and march, and in the stands are the prime minister of Israel and sixty thousand fans. So it's truly special to be a part of it. It's gotten bigger and bigger every year.

If I think back to the 1970s, it was probably nothing I imagined being part of, but as it grew I became more and more interested. And to be there in 2009 with my son and daughter was just a great scenario. My wife chose to stay home and take care of the dogs, which was the only negative. We would have had to board all five of our dogs, which would have been very expensive, and they probably wouldn't have spoken to us upon their return home.

What was also really fascinating was meeting Arabs who are part of the Druze religion. They serve in the Israeli army, and it was quite an experience to get to know them. They fed us and told us about their religion, and it was amazing—we thoroughly enjoyed that. And one of the biggest highlights was going to Masada, which overlooks the Dead Sea.

I guess of all the things we did, the most powerful was going to the Holocaust Museum called "Yad Vashem—The World Holocaust

Remembrance Center." There are many artifacts, and you can trace families and heritage. They even have a computer system on-site, so there are ways to check and see if you had any family members who were involved. It's incredibly moving, and to go through it is spectacular. The way it's put together is unbelievable, and every time we go back to Israel, it's one of the first things we do.

As for the soccer part of the trip, we didn't have a great team at all and had some real issues, ending up finishing fourth. We probably should've finished second or third. We beat Israel in pool play, making us the first US team to do that. We were playing Argentina in the semifinals, and the day before that, the parents took the kids to the beach and they got scorched. They were blistered and exhausted when we played again, and we got trounced. If we had stayed away from the beach and been rested, we would've done so much better. But that didn't happen, and we didn't do very well. The thing is the whole event is more than just games; it's an experience. We were housed at Kibbutz Shefayim, a large complex that had everything needed for not only our team but others as well. The highlight of each day was our nightly game of spades with my son, Adam Cooper, Ami Monson, me, and sometimes Barry Kaplan as a fourth when needed. We certainly enjoyed our time there.

Starting at the Maccabiah in 2009 gave me some insight into future games and how I wanted to really get involved with them from a coaching standpoint because I felt it was something that was so special. You don't find it anywhere else unless you go to the real Olympics or Pan-American Games. To be immersed in Israel and the heritage of Israel and to be with other Jewish people and coaches from around the world was just incredible.

The Games are about being back in Israel and its history. They call it "Coming Home," and what that means is that you're always welcome back in Israel—they want you there. They want to show you what's there. I have a dear friend through soccer named Roni Schneider who was with the Israeli Soccer Federation for years and played for their national team, and one day during an off day, we were invited to his home. Where he lived was within spitting distance of Jordan. One of my best friends in coaching, Adam Cooper, who coaches at Saint Mary's in California, was coaching the youth team and Barry Kaplan, who was coaching the girls' youth team, joined us, and we all went to Roni's house for lunch. The Maccabiah Games brought all that together.

I can't express how impactful the Games were to me and my family. We were able to go back and spend time in a country where we all came from at some point. Going there is special, and the icing on the cake is competing in the sport you love.

Chapter 23:
Maccabiah Gold—Part 1

AUSTRALIA STARTED HAVING ITS OWN MACCABIAH GAMES IN 2006, but it was under very difficult circumstances. It was held in the summer in that country—which is our winter—and it takes place during the Christmas season. So to compete in the Games there, you'd go on December 23 and not come home until after the first of the year. The last ones they hosted were in 2011, and that's when we went there. I had always wanted to go to Australia and took my daughter, and she was able to train and get ready to run in Israel.

As for soccer, we won the silver medal and had a great time. We played two teams from Australia, beat them, and then we played Brazil in our group and we beat them. After that we moved on to the knockout stage and played Mexico, a game we won. But as things turned out, we had to meet Brazil in the finals. Unfortunately, when we played them, we were exhausted. The leadership of our group decided the day before we'd go to the Blue Mountains and hike while Brazil was staying back at their hotel relaxing. So even though we beat them pretty handily in our group, they beat us 3–0 in the finals, and we had to settle for the silver medal. Our guys had no legs after hiking about nine miles, and our main guy was sick and throwing up, which made things difficult. But we still got to go to Australia and see a lot of different things, and it really was a fun trip overall. Since it was during the New Year's holiday, we got to witness an incredible fireworks display over Darling Harbor, and that was really a highlight. But beyond that the experience let me know what kind of players I'd need to look for if I got appointed to coach in any future Maccabiah Games. And I did. After that I had to bring in an assistant coach, and I found a really good one, which is an interesting story. His name is Warren Russ, and he's a great guy who I knew was really good at evaluating talent because he had helped us at one time when we were doing trials down in Florida for the 2009 juniors team. He was coaching at Georgia Southwestern University and had been there for about ten years and continued coaching there until 2019 when he decided to leave his position as the head men's soccer coach. So I thought he'd work out well as my assistant. Well, what I didn't realize at the time was that in our first game with the Grasshoppers back in 1993, we played the Orlando Lions and Warren was their goalkeeper. I talked to the program director and chairman of the soccer teams about appointing Warren as our assistant coach, and they made it official. I couldn't have had a better person and asset for our team than Warren.

So now that I had my assistant coach, it was time to start recruiting players to attend one of the tryouts, held in Philadelphia, Pennsylvania, and Los Angeles, California. The program director at Maccabi USA, Ami Monson, had a list of players he had accumulated over the years that we could start contacting. That was our first step, and then I started sending out emails to every coach in the NCAA—at all levels—asking for a list of Jewish athletes who might be interested. I needed their names and contact info. We recruited kids around the country. I think the tryout fee was $40, but when the first trials were held in Philadelphia, we had 131 players show up. We also recruited a couple other coaches to help evaluate the players. I wanted to see if they were going to be able to do the type of drills we do—the simple drills that I always did. I wanted to make sure they played simple instead of fancy and understood the way we coach and play, as well our system, to be successful.

There was one player there who was on the 2009 team named Scott Rowling. He had played at the University of New Hampshire and was a really good guy—good player and great leader. My goal was to bring him back with this team because that team in 2009 had some players who were just incredible. Their talent level was far superior to the talent level of our 2013 team, but they didn't mesh, mainly because they had some internal issues and finished fifth overall. Truthfully, they should have won because they had some really top talent but finished fifth. Guys like Benny Feilhaber, Jeff Agoos, Jonathan Bornstein, and some other really great players played on the 2005 team and only won the silver medal. So I knew we had our work cut out for us in order to try and win the gold medal. But what I had to do was interact with the players and see how they interacted with the other players. Plus, it was very important to me to see how they would react under different circumstances with players whom they'd never played with before. So we chose a really outstanding team, and I wanted Scott to be the captain and help the rest of the players to understand everything that went on in Israel during that time in 2009 and guide us a little.

A week after the trials in Philadelphia, we went to Los Angeles, and the numbers there were not as big as in Philadelphia—it was closer to fifty kids. But we chose six or seven players from that group including three players from the University of California at San Diego, Alec Arsht, Will Pleskow, and Adam Zernik, who really, along with Scott, ended up being the backbone of our team. One of our players was Daniel Kohen, who played for me in Australia and knew how I coached, so I named him cocaptain along with Scott. In trying to pick the team, I wasn't looking necessarily for the best players but players who I thought could give us the best chance to win because they all got along well. So each day after the trials, Warren and I would sit down and go through the players, and really in my mind I had already pretty much selected my team. We knew what school they'd played at and whether they started—we had all that documented because of all the recruiting I did prior to spending all that time every day evaluating players and looking at all the video I could find online to evaluate them even before our tryouts were held. So in my mind, unless something went seriously wrong, I already knew what the team would look like. I had to have players who I knew fit the team we wanted—emotionally, mentally, and physically. But I'm big on loyalty, so that factors in my decisions too. Three of the players I knew from our experience in Australia and one who played for me in 2009 were also selected. I selected them because I felt a sense of loyalty and they were outstanding players and people. There was a big striker out of Yale, Charlie Paris; a good defender out of a Division II school in Pennsylvania, Adam Green; and as I already mentioned, Daniel Kohen. The other player, Drew Rosenberg, an attacking midfielder, played for me in

2009 with our juniors team in Israel that finished fourth. Out of 131 players, we selected twenty, and we also had ten to fifteen alternates in case somebody got injured or dropped out for whatever reason, which inevitably happens. In fact, one of my best defenders was on a cruise with his parents and injured his wrist very badly playing basketball on the ship, so he had to drop out. Even so, we had a good group who went over there, and I knew we had a chance to do something with it if we could all stay cohesive. And that cohesiveness started the minute we boarded the plane. I loved that team. It was a team that got along and bought into the criteria I thought it would take for us to be successful.

We went early, and when we got over there, we started training and had some practice games against an Israeli club. They were a good club, and then we played another team from the area just to get us acclimated to play in the Games. We had only seven training sessions, so we had to make the most of our practices especially since we had never played together before. As part of the Israel Connect program, we got to get on the bus and go touring, and that made for a rather interesting time. We got to a beach area and just relaxed until we got back on our bus to continue our journey into the history of Israel and all the sights. The tour took us to all the famous places as we had done during the first time I was part of the Maccabiah Games. We went to the Dead Sea and the Wailing Wall and, of course, the Yad Vashem. We took part in the opening ceremony and being a part of that— wearing your Team USA clothing and standing together as a unit and seeing all the other nations there—is such a big deal. I think in 2013 there were seventy nations that were represented. Then we started our group play, which got off to a bad start, and I blame myself for that.

In our first game against Uruguay, they were diving and kicking us, and we weren't getting any kind of calls whatsoever. They were just playing for a tie, basically, because we really were a lot better than they were. But even worse was we were playing on this tiny field that I classified a postage stamp. Seriously, it was maybe 100 by 55, which is just ridiculous for a soccer field. It was awful. And I made a tactical mistake in that game. We had been working on playing a 4-5-1 so we could protect ourselves, but that field was too small to play in that system and didn't give us enough attack. We gave up a goal in the second half and lost 1–0. I was very upset, and I went to see the scheduling committee and went ballistic about the size of the field we had to play on. But when it was over, I told the players, "This one's on me. This was not your fault. I had you play-ing something we should have not been playing; even though we worked on it for seven sessions, we should've done something else under these conditions."

Most of the players had played a system that was either 4-4-2 or 4-3-3. I told them I wouldn't make that mistake again, but hopefully we wouldn't have to play on a field that narrow in future games. We had worked on a 3-5-2 system and would use it from now on and then fall back into our 4-5-1 after we got the lead. Now, because we lost, we had to win every game we played the rest of the way just to make it to the quarterfinal round. Our second game was against Denmark, and we destroyed them 5–0. That time the field was a little wider, so we decided to start in our 3-5-2 system to be more attack oriented. It worked, and the win was a great way to get us back on track and help us move forward to the next game, which was against Mexico.

When we had played them back in 2009, it was really physical and they spit on us and all kinds of things, but this was a different team—really well coached by Jacques Passy and with a lot of outstanding players. Their best man was a player named Allan Israel, who was the best striker I had ever coached against. He had played professionally for Atlante in the Mexican Premier Division and also for premier division Atlético Bucaramanga in Columbia. Allan was not only a great striker but one of the nicest people anyone could ever meet. We continue to stay in touch even to this day. That was our final game in the group, and we had to win it—a draw wouldn't have done us any good. So our guys knew it was win or we're out, going into the match.

We scored to make it 1–0 when our attacking mid received a great ball attacking down the right side and played a ball across to our striker, Jake Pace, who finished it nicely. Then Allan scored the first goal against us with just a rocket off his left foot to tie the game. After that, we scored on a great goal by Kovi Konowiecki to go up 2–1 just before halftime. They came back in the second half on another goal by Allan off a free kick to make it 2–2. But I think around the seventieth minute, my left back got the ball after a throw-in and he was maybe forty yards out and sent the ball into the upper 90 with his left foot to make it 3–2. I mean, it was on a rope. At that point we dropped back into a 4-5-1 to defend, and we wound up holding the lead and beating Mexico.

Then we had to play Germany in the quarterfinals; they had beaten Great Britain in a major upset to win their group. For some reason, their coach came out and played a 5-3-2 and I thought, "Holy cow! We can really take advantage of that." So we stayed at our 3-5-2 and just spread it out and ended up winning 7–0. At that point I decided to nickname our team the "A Train" after the Duke Ellington song, because we just kept rolling along. But once we got through them, we had to play Canada in the semifinals, and they had some phenomenal players—a lot of them were playing college ball in the United States and some had made it to the Canadian national team. We were predicted to get beat. In fact, the guy who had blackballed me many years before and was now on the Maccabiah Games executive committee came up to me before the game and wished me luck but basically said we didn't have a chance. I told him he was entitled to his opinion but I didn't agree with it. And it was not the correct opinion because we beat Canada 5–0. After the Mexico game, I really felt like the team had come together with the common goal of winning it all, and the Germany and Canada games really showed that they had become the "A Train." In the seventy-six-year history of the Maccabiah Games, no US men's team had won a gold medal in soccer, and to do that we had to beat the defending champions, Argentina, in the finals. They were very much a Latin team, in the sense that they were very physical, and we knew it would be an interesting game.

We went up 1–0 early from a long throw-in by Ross Friedman to Alec Arsht, who put it in the back of the net. Not long after that, they got a phantom penalty kick. It was awful, but they got the PK to make it 1–1. That was the score at halftime, and we made a few adjustments to our attack, trying to take away their space. Six minutes into the second half, we scored to make it 2–1, again off another long throw-in by Ross Friedman to Eric Weberman, who finished it nicely. But in the sixtieth minute, one of our guys—a great player out of Wake Forest, Kovi Konowiecki—got red carded, and we got down to ten men, losing one of our workhorses in the midfield. He got shoved to the ground and got up and shoved back, which is what the referee saw, so he got ejected. We had talked before the game about not getting baited, but we got baited.

So we were down a man and had to play the last thirty minutes with ten men, and we decided to shift to a 4-5-1 to try to keep hold of the game. But they scored and made it 2–2, so at that point we were hoping to make it to penalty kicks because that's where I thought we had an advantage. So regulation ended 2–2, and we played two overtime periods with no score, even though we had a couple of chances and they had a couple of chances. Fortunately, our keeper, Jacob Lissek, came up big.

We played the last sixty minutes with a man down, which was the gutsiest performance of any team I have ever coached. It allowed us to get to PKs, but our first kicker Adam Zernik missed, and he was our specialist on PKs. Then their guy missed his PK, so we were back to being even. We finally got to the point where it was 3–3 in PKs and if we made ours, we'd win. Scott had been hurt and told me before we started penalty kicks he didn't want to be part of the PKs, but I told him, "I don't care what you want; if it comes down to the fifth kick, you're taking it." And it did, and he made a beautiful kick that went right in the goal, giving us a 4–3 win on penalty kicks and giving the United States our first gold medal in men's soccer. We call that the "Impossible Dream Team" because no one ever gave us a chance; we simply didn't have the best players, just the hardest working and best people. And the level of play was so much higher—some of those teams could've come over here and beat MLS teams. But we just played our game—peanut butter and jelly sandwich on white bread with a glass of milk. By playing simply, the way I teach all my teams to play, we attained the impossible. And no matter what happens to the guys on that team for the rest of their lives, they'll always know that they were the first. They did what practically no one gave them any chance to do, and they did it because they played for each other. My philosophy that a great offense makes for a great defense came true. We scored twenty-two goals and only gave up five in six games.

This was our "Impossible Dream Team": Max Kurtzman, goalkeeper; Jacob Lissek, goalkeeper; Alec Arsht, defender; Ross Friedman, defender; Daniel Kohen, defender; Will Pleskow, midfielder; Ryan Jones, defender; Adam Green, defender; David

Abidor, midfielder; Eric Weberman, striker; Kovi Konowiecki, midfielder; Evin Nadaner, midfielder; Scott Rowling, midfielder; Gary Weisbaum, midfielder; Adam Zernik, midfielder; Drew Rosenberg, midfielder; Charlie Paris, striker; Matthew Kadoch, striker; Jake Pace, striker; David Rosenthal, striker.

Chapter 24:
Maccabiah Gold—Part 2

IT TRULY WAS A VERY DIFFICULT DECISION FOR ME TO GO BACK TO the Maccabiah Games again. How do I top what had already been done in being part of the first men's soccer team from the United States to win the gold medal? But the way it played out was interesting.

I had appointed my assistant, Warren Russ, to take over and be the head coach of the 2017 team, and he accepted that position. My good friend Mark Knue was the cochairman, along with me on Maccabi USA, so I still had ties to it. Plus, he and I had become great friends and remain so to this day. Well, as I've said before, Warren is very laid back and just a low-key kind of guy and that was why he and I worked so well together, but Mark called and said, "Look, you're going to have to take over" but didn't say why. It wasn't until later that I found out the reason. I told Mark I wasn't going to do that to Warren because he was too good a friend and had been instrumental in helping us in 2013. But Mark said he had already talked to him and Warren wanted me as well. I said if I talk to Warren and get the sense he's hurt by it, I'm not going. But if he wants me to take over, I will. A few hours later, I got a call from Warren, and he was really sincere and said he just wasn't up to doing it because he was having some health issues. He did agree to go as my assistant, though, as long as his health held out. At that point I decided I'd do it, but we were about six months behind in recruiting; so we were already in a tough spot right from the start.

When I coached in 2013, I had already started recruiting in March and April, and this time it was August and the Games were coming up. Warren just didn't have the energy to recruit, so I had to get it done in a short period of time. So I started recruiting and spending hours every day doing it, trying to find players and begging coaches to tell me about any Jewish players they might have who would be interested. I was making all sorts of calls to as many coaches and players I could think of. And I also had my previous list to go by. However, I really didn't want to go back because I just didn't think we could duplicate what we accomplished in 2013. That was such a special team, winning the championship game by playing a man down for thirty minutes of regulation and thirty minutes of overtime. More than likely that was the gutsiest performance of any team I've ever been associated with, and how do you duplicate that? How do you even come close? Even my wife said it was a bad idea for those same reasons. Plus, I didn't know who would show up at the tryouts and who I'd get. But then I thought to myself, "Well, maybe I can top it if we could become the first US team to go back-to-back with the same coach." Israel's won the Maccabiah Games multiple times, but never consecutively with the same coach. So I thought that if I could get four or five players from that 2013 team, maybe we could still do something special. That was the new goal.

But I started recruiting, and the numbers were not right. I think we had seventy-one show up in Philadelphia, which was about sixty-something less than we had in 2013, and we only had maybe thirty show up for our California tryouts. And some of them didn't come back for a second or third session, so the numbers dropped. I think we got down to twenty-four players in California on the last day we were there. It was a difficult situation for us to try and find these players, and that's why it became vital that I find players from 2013 to help build the bridge between me and the new team. We needed them to show the new players how we do things on and off the field and what the new players can expect during this time over there from a fatigue standpoint. The returning players I chose were

Evin Nadaner, our defensive midfielder; Kovi Konowiecki, our center midfielder; Max Kurtzman, our goalkeeper; Daniel Kohen, one of our center backs; and Ryan Jones, our outside back. These five players would be an integral part of our success.

And as it turned out, I really didn't have an assistant coach because after the tryouts Warren got really sick. But he had coached the Maccabi team in Chile at the Pan-American Games a year before, and he said there was a guy there named David Goldstein who wanted to coach. He graduated from Princeton and had been a student assistant with them, and he was a really good guy. So it turned out OK for us. It wasn't what I wanted because I wanted Warren with me again, but David did a great job for us.

I had two trainers earlier who I thought would want to help during the Maccabiah Games. They weren't Jewish, but that doesn't matter when it comes to trainers. So I could pick who I wanted. The one I wanted the most was a guy named Kyle Southall and the other was Daniel Lindsey, and both of them got to go to Israel. Kyle ended up working with our team and helping others if they needed it, and Daniel worked with the Masters teams in the Games. And let me tell you—Kyle is perhaps the best athletic trainer I've ever been around in my entire career. He's incredible at both diagnosing and treating on the spot. He was a trainer for me at Birmingham-Southern, so I knew what he was capable of. Since we couldn't train, after the games Kyle would take players to the pool to regenerate and recover. They might also play soccer tennis something like that, but the main thing was getting in the pool and regenerating their bodies with stretching. The guys loved him and I'm not sure we could've kept our players healthy enough to compete without Kyle. That's how important he was to us.

We had less training than we did in 2013 because the heat was so intense. This time they canceled everything because the heat index was well over 105 degrees, so they stopped us from training. That meant going in we had less than seven training sessions total and our scrimmage games we had arranged with Mexico and one other team had to be cancelled. We ended up playing our youth team one evening, but after sixty minutes we were destroying them and we just weren't getting anything out of it. So we ended it right then. We were staying in Ramat Gan, just outside Tel Aviv. We were still able to go touring and bond as a team, but as it wears you out, you have to be extremely careful.

We had a very difficult group. While we were the number one seed (because we were the defending champions), the group included Great Britain, who were a very talented team, along with Venezuela and Australia. Great Britain had been upset in 2013 by

Germany, but a lot of people expected they'd win it in 2017 if Israel

didn't. In fact, they play as the London Lions in one of the lower

divisions in the English football pyramid. Great Britain won their

first game against Australia, and we won our first game against

Venezuela 3–0. That was probably the dirtiest team I've ever coached

against. They were kicking our guys' legs bloody and threatened to

come to our hotel after the game and fight us. In fact, we almost

had a fight right after the game. And what made matters worse in

the Maccabiah Games is that many opposing teams traveled to and

from games together. We were supposed to be on the bus with them

going back, and that would've been a disaster.

Mark was there along with his family and friends touring

Israel, and one of the friends with him was former NFL player

Cris Collinsworth. They arranged transportation on their bus and

offered us a ride because otherwise it would've been a bloodbath.

Our next game was against Great Britain, and we knew we had

our work cut out for us. We were playing our backup keeper, Josh

Haberman, who was really good and played well, but with about

four minutes left in the game, they got a corner kick. One of their

players was left unmarked, and they got one past our goalkeeper to

make it 1–0, which is how the game ended. We had some chances,

and they had some chances. They put away the ball that they had to put away, but we didn't do what we were supposed to do. We always play man-to-man on corners, but I always put two players on the edge of the 6 (6-yard box in front of the goal line), one at the front and one at the back. They play using a zonal-marking system and are free to pick up any player who comes free into their area, either by coming from the backside or from losing one of our players marking them. Well, they didn't pick up this guy, so we lost and our backs were up against the wall once again. It didn't happen in the first game like it did in 2013; it happened in the second, but either way we had to win every game just to get to the quarterfinals again.

Our next game was against Australia, and they were much better in 2017 than they were in 2013. It was a battle but we beat them 2–0, even though I thought we should've won by more and should've put them away fairly easily. But we didn't have any training facilities to speak off, so we never had any training between games. That's why you need a great trainer, and we had him in Kyle.

After we beat Australia, we went to the quarterfinals and who should we play but Uruguay, the team that beat us in 2013. This time, though, we just destroyed them from the start, going up 4–0 and ending up beating them 4–2. After that we were able to watch the last half of the Israel and Argentina game to see who we'd get in the semifinals, and it was Israel. We were hoping Argentina would win because Israel was the under-23 national team and they were really good. Israel won on penalty kicks, and we got to watch how they took them and study them before our game.

It turned out we had to play them on a postage-stamp field, and they also put us in a small locker room with no air conditioning. They did that on purpose; I firmly believe that. It didn't even have enough chairs for all of us to sit down, and there was no bathroom in there. There were other dressing rooms at that complex we could've used, but they did this I guess to intimidate us or something; we were pissed off.

We went out in a 3-5-2. I thought we have our best team on the field, but we got down 1–0 in the first half. My center mid just wasn't having a good day. He sent a ball back toward our goal and kicked it so hard it ricocheted off one of our guys and went right to a striker from Israel and they scored. We made some changes at halftime and decided we were going to attack them by pushing people forward and trying to get the equalizer. We felt like their backs were slow and susceptible to the counterattack and that we could get around them, and sure enough, it worked. I told them we had to get a couple of goals early before we could sit back and pick and choose what we needed to do. We started out in a 3-5-2, and Alec Weiss scored off a great assist from Stephen Elias to tie the game four minutes into the second half. Our goalkeeper, Max Kurtzman, really kept us in the game with great play and helped us weather the storm. He was just unbelievable. So with the score at 1–1, I decided to drop back into our 4-5-1 formation and hoped we could keep the score that way and get a penalty kick opportunity at the end of the second half.

I had two guys who could throw the ball in extremely well. Daniel Kohen, from our 2013 team, took the throw, and it came inside the box where Lance Dotzman went up and headed the ball into the goal to put us ahead 2–1. The only problem was he broke his nose when he collided with a player on the other team, and it was a bloody mess. That goal came in the fifty-eighth minute, and we went in front 2–1, but we lost Lance. He was bleeding pretty badly and didn't look good at all. After that Israel just made an onslaught trying to tie things up, but we defended like crazy. Max made save after save, and we hung on and got the win. So I started to think we might be a destiny team here, because we hung on against the best team in the tournament and one that probably should've had four or five goals against us. Winning that game was unbelievable. After the game there was a TV spot where they interviewed the Israeli coach, and they asked him how they lost the game to a team like us. He said they shouldn't have lost, that they should've been up by several goals. But he said that we had made some critical tactical changes and they didn't adjust to that and that's why we won. And that made me feel good, knowing we could make necessary changes when we had to make them.

Our win meant we were going to the finals, and we were going to play Great Britain again. They were confident, but we had learned a lot about them the first time we played. I felt that if we attacked their right back, we could get around him and score goals. But their strikers were huge—just big, strong strikers. They were a typical English team, kick and run, big boys up top, big boys in the back—except on that right side. Well, to start the game, they came right down the field and hit the crossbar with their first shot, and I thought, "Oh my God, we're in trouble." We just started off really flat for some reason. About three-fourths of the way through the first half, they got a breakaway. Max came out after the ball, and they made contact. Max got smacked in the head with the guy's boot—he didn't get the ball, just Max's head—and he got automatically ejected. So it's kind of déjà vu in reverse for us, in that we're going to play a man up now as opposed to a man down for the remainder of the half. And we ended up scoring to make it 1–0 before halftime. So at 1–0 we're going to stay in our 3-5-2, but before the game I made a decision unlike any decision I'd ever made in coaching.

I took out one of my captains, Kovi Konowiecki. Kovi was the center mid, and my attacking mid was Jake Rozhansky, who had won a national championship at Virginia and then transferred to Maryland. I moved Jake, who had scored our first goal, to left wing. I wanted him to take on their right back, who I believed was their weakest player in the back. So we played without a center mid and really without an attacking mid. My defensive mid was a player who played for me back in 2013 and was the MVP of the tournament, Evin Nadaner, and he really stepped up both defensively and offensively. My right-wing player, Steven Elias, came in a lot and got in the middle to play balls for us. I told my team before the game we were going to do something very unconventional and we did. As it turned out, Jake scored two more goals, and we won 3–0 because he attacked their right back, who we thought was their weakest back and get around him.

He could cut in on his right foot and finish the ball—I always like my left wings to be right footed and my right wings to the left footed—because they can cut in on the ball with their dominant foot.

That change is what propelled us to win the game. Had we played conventionally with our attacking mid, center mid, and defensive mid, I'm not sure we would've been able to win the game because they were so big and strong, and I don't think we could've matched them as the game progressed. But that change not only gave us our best chance of winning but it also created what I had been striving for my entire career—a perfect game. While it wasn't for the entire ninety minutes, it was for about eighty minutes and in having a second half as close to a perfect game as I've ever coached in. The first half was one where we thought we were going to hold on because we had a lead, but the second half was as close to a perfect half as I have ever been a part of. It was what I had been looking for my entire career. We made very few unforced errors and kept possession of the ball. We played perfect balls to feet. That's the way you play the game, with the ball on the ground and move off the ball. We played to our strengths. I had a perfect team to execute that perfection, and it was as close to perfection as you're ever going to get. Max had some big saves, but there was nothing in the second half that they could do once we were up 3–0. When that final whistle went off and we won that game I thought to myself, "That's the first time in my long career that I've come as close to coaching a team to perfection."

I don't think anyone will ever see the likes of that kind of a game or for that matter a team that truly cared about each other and executed our philosophy and system to perfection like our 2017 gold-medal-winning team again in Israel. No one could ever think we could win the way we did by transforming our team to play in the most unconventional system, but because of these play-ers, I knew we could and we did. And that was my goal going over there—I wanted to coach a team that I felt could do what we wanted them to do, to be as close to perfection as possible. No one could believe I took out my center mid—a great player and a great kid—but it was the tactical decision we had to make to have a chance to win the game. Prior to the game, I told him he wasn't starting, and I'm sure it hurt him. But I explained the reasons behind it, and he understood because he knew the team came first and he was a team player. After the game I told them that just like my 2013 team was the first to win the gold medal for the US men, they were really part of a "first" too, because we were the first to go back-to-back in the Maccabiah Games with the same coach. Just like Neil Armstrong was the first person to step on the moon, Buzz Aldrin was the second man to step on the moon but part of the first crew. That 2013 team was the "Impossible Dream Team," but this one was the "Forever Team," because I don't believe that anyone will duplicate what they did. And no one can ever take that away from them.

This time there were eighty countries represented and over ten thousand athletes there. There were sixteen teams in the tourna-ment, so the competition level was extremely high. And as for my favorite, I could never choose between the 2013 and 2017 teams. It was spectacular. I mean I couldn't have drawn or written out the end of my career any better than that. That is a storybook ending. I guess it's tenacity of purpose—being tenacious enough with what you want to accomplish and being able to get the players to buy into that passion and that purpose. I think it was the most special thing I've ever been a part of in my career. And I had a quote for the team. I said, "Hope becomes reality when enthusiasm finds the opportunities and energy makes the most out of them."

All the stars aligned perfectly for that last team, and I got to go out a winner. Here are the players who helped us in our record-setting win:

Max Kurtzman, goalkeeper; Josh Haberman, goalkeeper; Ryan Jones, defender; Daniel Kohen, defender; Benjamin Issroff, defender; Jonny Dolezal, defender; Sam Raben, defender; Daniel Rubenstein, defender; Elijah Lichtenberg, defender; William Cohen, defender; Evin Nadaner, midfielder; Kovi Konowiecki, midfielder; Jake Rozhansky, midfielder; Aaron Franco, midfielder; Lance Dotzman, midfielder; Sam Friedman, midfielder; Brett Walsdorf, midfielder; Alec Weiss, striker; Stephen Elias, striker; Oliver Eisen, striker.

I would be remiss to not thank our entire staff who made this journey a reality. Besides Kyle Southall there were two other trainers who helped us—Daniel Lindsey and Hayley Edenzon. Our team doctors, Dr. David Rubenstein and Dr. Michael April, were so valuable to our team, along with our chairman of soccer and my dear friend, Mark Knue, for without him and his guidance, none if this would have been possible. Lastly, Steve Graber, Lou Moyerman, and Dan Kurtz, all from Maccabi USA organization, were also extremely vital to our team and our incredible success. I thank you all from the bottom of my heart, and I will be forever grateful to each of you.

Chapter 25:
How I Coached the Game

SYSTEM OF PLAY: OUR 3-5-2: THE game of soccer is really quite simple. As you know by now if you've read through this book, we're not interested in caviar but rather peanut butter and jelly sandwich on white bread with a glass of milk. What that means is that we are not interested in anything fancy, only basic fundamental soccer. "Conservative with a pinch of flair" best describes our game. You create that style of play with "excellence through fundamentals." There are no superstars on this team. Only the team is the superstar.

The game of soccer is based totally on movement off the ball and the ability to think. In other words, you must possess the ability to see the play before you receive the ball, know what you want to do with the ball after receiving it, and know where you must go after the pass is made. This is simple soccer, which is a game of one- or two-touch passing, movement continuously off the ball, communication constantly, and the ability to attack an opponent and go to goal once in our attacking box.

You must be committed to perform these functions and have total belief in it. It requires 100 percent effort at all times, thus striving for perfection—always knowing it is unattainable but knowing the drop from 100 percent is less if you start with perfection.

Let us now look at our system of play and how we are successful with it. This system allows us to be conservative yet creative enough to have a "pinch of flair." Our system will obviously change based on our players and what the opposition is doing during the course of the game. We will always be a possession-oriented team, and believing and trusting in our philosophy is a must for the entire team. If everyone is committed to the game plan and tactics, we can be very successful. But it takes everyone being on the same page, day in and day out.

Goalkeeper: Last line of defense and the first one in the attack. Must constantly communicate with defenders and midfielders on defense. Must also be readily available for pass back to control pace and tempo of the game in our buildup. This allows us an outlet to change the ball from one side to the other. Very seldom punts the ball. It is done only in certain situations during the game. Mostly to launch a quick counterattack and also when the field is not suitable for playing a possession game on the ground. Also sometimes to delay the game.

Sweeper: Very conventional play, with the ability to get forward in the attack as an element of surprise. Controls the defense and should almost always be free. He must be able to step up and pick up the opponent if he gets free on counterattack and be able to mark him to stop the opponent's progress. He must always play behind the marking backs unless he has to step to the man or when he is going forward on the attack. However, if he goes forward, there must be a midfielder to change positions with him until he can get back in position.

Marking Backs: Play strictly man-to-man defense. Always mark opponent's strikers. We never leave our men at any time! No switching unless as last resort. Never leave your man in the defensive third of the field to pick up a 1 v 1 situation. Let the goalkeeper come and close the angle. Marking backs never take throw-ins in the defensive third of the field.

Wing Midfielders: Must be willing and able to run from end line to end line. They act as fourth and fifth defenders in the defensive third of the field and act as fourth and fifth midfielders in the middle and attacking third of the field. They must always give width to the attack by playing on the touchlines. They must be the fittest players on the team and understand the importance and necessity of the position in our systems.

Defensive Midfielder: Acts as a windshield wiper, sweeping up in front of the defense. Can and must go forward on well-timed runs into the attacking third. Normally, will mark the opponents' most dangerous midfielder. Plays somewhat like a stopper in a 4-4-2 system but with a great deal more range in the attack. Always gives support around the ball in the buildup phase of our system, thus creating the triangle effect around the ball in the defensive third of the field.

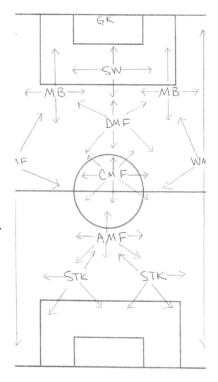

Center Midfielder: The field general. The go-to player in the middle of the field. He dictates the pace and tempo or rhythm of our team. He, like the defensive mid-fielder, is readily around the ball at all times in the defensive third of the field. He must always dictate that the ball not bypass the midfield, by demanding possession of it from the defenders when applicable. He is always giving support around the ball and will get the ball very quickly from the defenders. He is always in the attack as well. He gives support to the attacking midfielder, wing midfielders, and strikers. He also makes very well-timed runs into the attacking third of the field and is always able to get back in the defense and behind the ball very quickly. He is the playmaker on the team! He must also be able to hold the ball under pressure in order to give the team a chance to get organized in the attack or buildup.

Attacking Midfielder: Plays somewhat like a third or withdrawn striker. He creates the one-two opportunities with the strikers. He must also always get back in the defense once possession is lost. He always supports both strikers. He must be capable of holding the ball in pressure situations as well.

Strikers: Must be able to play with their backs to the goal and be able to hold the ball until support arrives. This must be done under extreme pressure. They must have constant movement on and off the ball to create scoring opportunities. They must be willing to mark the overlapping backs and come back into the defense. They also dictate our high-pressure defense once we lose possession in our attaching third. One striker will always put pressure on the ball, and the other striker will try to cut off the back pass.

Organizational form of the 3-5-2 system:

The emphasis here is on the buildup once we have possession. The only disadvantage of this system is when our wing midfield players are in the defense creating five defensive players and we regain possession and give our wing midfielders a chance to get back into the support and attach roles. This is especially true for the strikers who must have extremely good positional play in relation to each other, the midfielders, and defenders. Obviously, the outside midfielders must possess a great deal of physical and buildup qualities to negate the disadvantage during buildup after possession is regained.

Thus our defenders must play the ball directly to our central midfielders who are our most creative players. They can also play the ball to our wing midfielders as they become a very important link to this buildup either as support to the defenders or as outlets in order to get the attack started. These outside midfielders or wing midfielders must be very good and quick in the transition from defense to offense.

Most important to this system's transition from defense to offense is a very slow buildup to allow our players to get better organized and have numbers around the ball. Our sweeper must be the key to this happening.

Within the system, we must understand three basic principles: *balance, rhythm,* and *flow.*

Balance: Finding the right place for our players will create our balance through our organization and positional play to better transition the ball, thus creating our rhythm.

Rhythm: Created and dictated by the transition from defense to offense. It's a slow buildup, allowing all players to get organized and allowing the ball to transition from defense through the midfield to the strikers. This creates our flow.

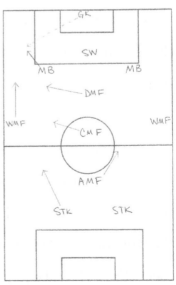

Flow: From the balance and rhythm in our buildup and transition, we create our flow or rather our team possession game!

The 3-5-2 system we play is a combination of possession and

buildup soccer and a play-making style with the element of surprise counterattack!

This is like going to a symphony, where all the musicians are placed accordingly and are warming up with a lot of noise. Then the conductor taps his wand, and it all comes together in a beautiful sound.

In order for us to be a possession-oriented team, there must be ball circulation, fast combination play, and positional play. These are critical to the system. One- and two-touch passing is a must. This system of buildup or play making can also be used to apply pressure on the opponent. That is, when we lose possession in our own attacking third, we can apply immediate and relentless pressure on the opponent, trying to disrupt their rhythm and win possession back in our own half of the field.

Good midfield play is essential to our system. The midfield is the secondary line of defense and cannot create vulnerability. They must stay disciplined. Secondary runs are crucial as movements off the ball are the bread and butter of our system.

Attacking on the flanks is also vital with the wing midfielders being able to cross a proper and well-timed ball into the box, always remembering to take the keeper out of the play by where we cross the ball. Most space is available on the flanks, so we must utilize them effectively and often.

Now, how do we begin the buildup?

We must first get possession of the ball. Then we have to create numbers around the ball, or triangles. Thus, that will always give us at least two options to play to. The wing midfielder will come back to support the defenders, as will the central midfielders. The strikers must show in the midfield. One-twos are a must to beat any and all pressure. We can also slow the game down while maintaining possession by taking the ball back around the back to change the point of attack. This is accomplished by using the keeper or sweeper to change sides with the ball, thus still maintaining possession while the ball advances forward.

In the middle third of the field until the final forty yards, we will play a *drop, shift,* and *cover* defense. This is a zonal-marking system with man-to-man principles. Once we fall back to forty yards, we

Defensive third ⟶

Middle third ⟶

Attacking third ⟶

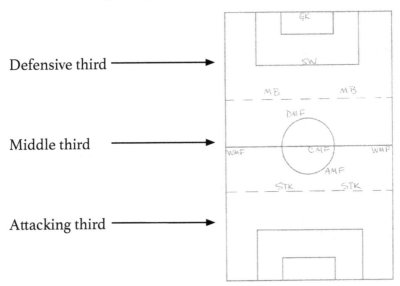

play strictly man-to-man defense in the final third. There must be great communication and vision in this drop, shift, and cover system in the middle third of the field.

Set Pieces:

Defensive walls:

Always set by the goalkeeper in numbers and placement. The mark is always on the sweeper. We never have our marking backs in the defensive walls.

Defensive corners:

One always on the front post and normally one on the back post. Everyone is goal side and man to man. We always send one out to mark their short corners.

Corner Kicks:

We have four corner kicks. We have one player on front post and three players at the top of the penalty box, making runs into the area. We always have our wing midfielder from the opposite side at the top of the arc or a little behind it to prevent any counterattack off the corner.

   No. 1: Far post for header

No. 2: Flick. Drive the ball to front-post man who then flicks the ball backward to one of our players to score. The flick will always freeze the goalkeeper.

No. 3: Short corner. Front post will run out to receive the ball and play back to corner taker for either a cross to back post or even a shot.

No. 4: Low-driven ball between goal line and 6-yard box, trying to get a misdirected ball in the goal.

Corner Kick Diagrams:

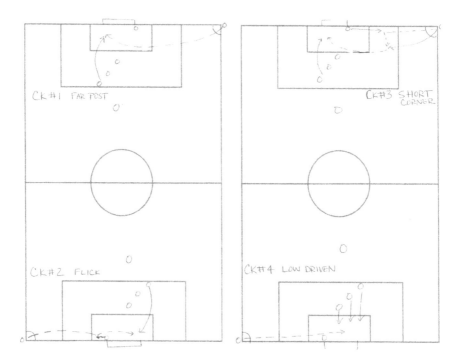

Free Kicks:

We always use the same formation on all our free kicks. That is, we have three players around the ball and always two players on the corners of their wall. We also have one player on the opposite side from the ball.

Play No. 1: Player 1 passes to player 2 who stops the ball, and player 3 runs up and shoots.

Play No. 2 Brehme (who was a German National player after which this play was designed) 1 passes to player 2 who stops the ball. Player 3 is running up as in play 1, but player 1 steps to the ball he passed and shoots.

Play No. 3 Hammer: Player 1 passes to player 2. Player 2 stops the ball for a split second. Player 1 acts like he is going to shoot, but player 2 passes the ball behind him for player 3 to shoot.

Play No. 4 Heel: Player 1 acts like he is passing the ball to player 2 but steps over the ball and heels the ball behind him for player 3 to shoot.

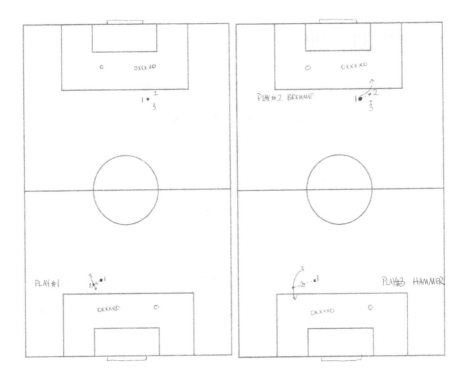

Play No. 5 Brehme with cross: Player 1 passes to player 2. Player 2 stops the ball, and player 3 runs up as if he is going to shoot. Player 1 steps up to strike the ball but crosses to the player on the opposite side for header on goal.

Play '94: Player 1 passes to player 2. Player 2 stops the ball, and player 3 runs up as if he is going to shoot. Player 1 then steps to strike the ball but passes just outside the wall to striker in the wall on the opposite side, running behind the wall to receive and shoot.

Play Loopfa: Player 1 chips ball over the wall to our striker, turning around to receive the ball for volley or half volley.

Nine Keys to Winning:

1. Combination play that's effective and dangerous, with possession-based passing built out of the back.

2. Central area penetrating passes.

3. Attacking from the outside backs.

4. Selfless high-speed off-the-ball movement to offer passing options.

5. Very fast, effective counters with fast transition through the midfield.

6. High-tempo play used to force errors, with intense pressure to regain possession. This is the go-to pressure system.

7. Effective driven crosses with outswingers or inswingers when possible.

8. High defensive line with an alert goalkeeper.

9. Defensive line set by the backs in order to maintain a thirty-five-meter distance to the strikers.

If we can concentrate on these nine principles to winning, we can accomplish our goals! We must all be selfless in our drive to succeed, with one common principle—readiness both mentally and physically.

"Hope becomes reality when enthusiasm finds the opportunities and energy makes the most out of them!"

Thank You

First and foremost, I want to thank Scott Adamson for being the guiding light in helping me put this book on paper. He has been such a great mentor along this journey! I also want to thank all my former coaches, who were my mentors in my coaching career. I also want to thank my administration at BSC and Maccabi USA, as well as my assistant coaches, especially Greg Vinson, and athletic trainers. In closing, I thank all my players throughout my thirty-three-year career at BSC and the two gold-medal-winning players on our Impossible Dream and Forever Teams of 2013 and 2017!

In closing my journey through this book, I would like to paraphrase Sir Winston Churchill and say, "Never has one person owed so much to so many."

Year-by-Year Records

Birmingham-Southern College (BSC) 363-250-52

1983: 4-14-0

1984: 9-9-1

1985: 16-8-0

1986: 15-5-5

1987: 11-6-1

1988: 8-5-4

1989: 14-6-0

1990: 14-6-1

1991: 9-9-2

1992: 7-11-2

1993: 8-11-3

1994: 16-5-0

1995: 21-3-1

1996: 17-6-2

1997: 17-4-1

1998: 14-5-3

1999: 19-6-1

2000: 12-10-0

2001: 6-12-1

2002: 5-12-2

2003: 12-5-4

2004: 12-7-0

2005: 12-5-1

2006: 6-10-1 *year college

    eliminated D1

2007: 10-10-0

2008: 4-16-0	2012: 6-5-2
2009: 11-6-2	2013: 9-8-1
2010: 5-9-4	2014: 13-4-1
2011: 10-7-0	2015: 11-5-2

Grasshoppers SC 37-29-1

1993: 7-6-0	1995: 11-9-1
1994: 16-5-0	1996: 3-9-0

Maccabiah Team USA 19-5-1

- 2009: Israel: Junior Team 4-2-1 fourth place
- 2010: Australia Maccabi Games: Open Men 5-1-0 silver medal
- 2013: Israel: Open Men 5-1-0 gold medal
- 2017: Israel: Open Men 5-1-0 gold medal
- Overall coaching record: 419-284-54

Summary:

BSC records: 363-250-52 with ten regular season championships, seven conference tournament championships, and four national tournament appearances with three final fours and one national runner-up. Coached two NAIA national players of the year. Coached first-ever USA gold-medal-winning team in the seventy-six-year history of the World Maccabiah Games in Israel, 2013. First-ever coach to win a gold medal in back-to-back World Maccabiah Games in 2017.

My overall coaching record is 414-284-53.

Conference Championships

1987, 1989, 1990, 1995, 1996, 1997, 1998, 1999, 2004, 2005

Conference Tournament Championships

1993, 1995, 1996, 1997, 1998, 1999, 2000

Maccabiah records

- 2009: 4-2-1 fourth-place finish
- 2010: 5-1-0 silver medal
- 2013: 5-1-0 gold medal, scoring twenty-two goals and giving up only five!
- USA v Uruguay 0–1; USA v Denmark 5–0; USA v Mexico 3–2; quarterfinals: USA v Germany 7–0; semifinals: USA v Canada

5–0; finals: USA v Argentina 2–2 and in PKs 4–3; we won the gold medal!

- 2017: 5-1-0 gold medal in back-to-back games. Fourteen goals for and four goals against. Beat Venezuela 3–0; lost to Great Britain 0–1; beat Australia 2–0; beat Uruguay 4–2 in quarterfinals; beat Israel 2–1 in semifinals; and beat Great Britain 3–0 in finals for the gold medal.

- Overall World Maccabiah record is 14-4-1 and complete Maccabi record including Australia Maccabi Games is 19-5-1.

- Overall record from 1993 to 1996 including Grasshoppers is 37-29-1.

- Overall coaching record is 419-284-53.

Pictures

1966 Shades Valley High School Varsity Basketball Team

*Chapter 3 Isadore Goldfarb, Fannye
Goldfarb, Morton Goldfarb and me.*

Marie and me at my BSC Hall of Fame induction.

Getting my 2nd LT.   *Surgeons Hands, UAB Hospital.*
Commission in 1972.

Dolphin on the Bow in Abaco, Bahamas.

The late Hardy Jones riding on an 18 foot wing span Manta Ray in the Sea of Cortez.

Getting a Yellow Card for yelling at the referee at BSC.

BSC Soccer after a very big win.

Coaching my BSC Team.

Getting my 350th win at BSC.

*Article on 1996 Olympic
Soccer coming to Birmingham,
AL and Legion Field.*

*My Soccer Staff and children
and pups from left to right
Sean McBride, Rui Menezes,
Greg Vinson, Aly Goldfarb
Paquette, Sean Goldfarb
and Satch and Cassie.*

*My last Excellence through
Fundamentals Soccer Camp at BSC*

*Aly Goldfarb Paquette,
Armin Kraaz and Sean
Goldfarb at my soccer camp*

The naming of the field, Preston Goldfarb Field at BSC.

*My Birmingham Grasshopper Team play-
ing in the Aloha Bowl, Honolulu, Hawaii.*

Marie and Me at my 350th win at BSC.

Our Golden Family, Marie with Max, Sean with Kol,
Aly with Kippi and me with Cassie and Satch.

My final team banquet at BSC.

Marie, me and Satch.

Our grandchildren, me with Fiona and Marie with Otis.

Our first Golden, Nesty.

*Our children in the back, Sammy
and Sean and Aly with Fiona and
her husband Jon with Otis.*

Sean, Sammy, Fiona and Otis.

2017 Double Gold Medal winning players left to right, Max Kurtzman, Kovi Konowiecki, me, Daniel Kohen, Ryan Jones and Evin Nadaner

2017 Back to Back Gold Medal Team

2013 first ever Maccabi USA Gold Medal Team.

CPSIA information can be obtained
at www.ICGtesting.com
Printed in the USA
BVHW041051301121
622865BV00020B/1017

9 781638 379492